BRIGHT NOTES

JANE EYRE BY CHARLOTTE BRONTË

Intelligent Education

Nashville, Tennessee

BRIGHT NOTES: Jane Eyre
www.BrightNotes.com

No part of this publication may be used or reproduced in any manner whatsoever without written permission, except in the case of brief quotations in critical articles and reviews. For permissions, contact Influence Publishers http://www.influencepublishers.com.

ISBN: 978-1-645420-60-6 (Paperback)
ISBN: 978-1-645420-61-3 (eBook)

Published in accordance with the U.S. Copyright Office Orphan Works and Mass Digitization report of the register of copyrights, June 2015.

Originally published by Monarch Press.
Ruth Harriett Blackburn; Margaret La Pointe, 1964
2019 Edition published by Influence Publishers.

Interior design by Lapiz Digital Services. Cover Design by Thinkpen Designs.

Printed in the United States of America.

Library of Congress Cataloging-in-Publication Data forthcoming.
Names: Intelligent Education
Title: BRIGHT NOTES: Jane Eyre
Subject: STU004000 STUDY AIDS / Book Notes

CONTENTS

1)	Introduction to Charlotte Brontë	1
2)	Introduction to Charlotte Brontë Life Of Charlotte Brontë	9
3)	Background	35
4)	Important Features	40
5)	Textual Analysis	
	Chapter 1	45
	Chapter 2	48
	Chapter 3	51
	Chapter 4	53
	Chapter 5	57
	Chapter 6	59
	Chapter 7	61
	Chapter 8	63
	Chapter 9	65
	Chapter 10	67
	Chapter 11	69
	Chapter 12	71
	Chapter 13	74
	Chapter 14	76

Chapter 15	78
Chapter 16	80
Chapter 17	82
Chapter 18	84
Chapter 19	86
Chapter 20	89
Chapter 21	92
Chapter 22	94
Chapter 23	96
Chapter 24	98
Chapter 25	100
Chapter 26	102
Chapter 27	105
Chapter 28	108
Chapter 29	111
Chapter 30	112
Chapter 31	114
Chapter 32	116
Chapter 33	118
Chapter 34	120
Chapter 35	122
Chapter 36	124
Chapter 37	126
Chapter 38	128
Conclusion	130
Character Analyses	132
Survey Of Criticism	150
Essay Questions And Answers	165
Suggestions For Further Study And Research	171
Bibliography	174

INTRODUCTION TO CHARLOTTE BRONTË

THE BRONTËS

The four Brontës lived and died in the first part of the nineteenth century. They were born in the years just after the Napoleonic wars - Charlotte the year after Waterloo (1815), the victory of her hero, the Duke of Wellington. Branwell, Emily, and Anne saw the first dozen years of Queen Victoria's long reign (1837–1901). Only Charlotte lived to see the mid-century mark and the Great Exhibition of 1851 (the ancestor of our World's Fair), which celebrated half a century of progress.

These were years of swift and kaleidoscopic change in England. Few periods have seen such changes in the face of a country in such a short time. Though there had long been some industrial centers, England in the early years of the nineteenth century was still predominantly rural. The majority of the people were in some way connected with the land, and the typical community was the village with its parson and squire (local landed proprietor). Land was what counted in terms of power and prestige. Landowning gentry such as Rochester in *Jane Eyre*, the Lintons in *Wuthering Heights*, and Darcy and Bingley in Jane Austen's *Pride and Prejudice*, were important socially and politically.

But already by the year of Waterloo, industry was growing rapidly and more and more communities became large slums. Great cotton mills had sprung up in Lancashire and with them coal mines and blast furnaces. Steam-driven machinery was installed in Yorkshire; the traditional wool industry began to feel the effects of the Industrial Revolution, and enterprising mill-owners began to buy the new machinery. Power spinning began to drive out hand spinning. Side by side with mechanized industry came better transportation. Already the roads had been greatly improved and the construction of canals begun. Coaches and barges went everywhere. In 1825, when the Brontës were small children, the first railway was built; by the time they were young people, and had a small legacy to invest, the railways offered them a good return on their money and the great iron web was spreading all over the land, taking new thoughts and new ideas as well as new goods wherever it went.

It is interesting to notice, though, that while Charlotte and Emily Brontë were in advance of their time in their independent habits of mind, they liked to place their stories in the past. The opening chapter of *Wuthering Heights* is dated 1802, and the main action of the story begins a generation before that. Charlotte's *Shirley* deals with the Luddite riots - outbreaks of machine-smashing by unemployed factory workers - which took place during the Napoleonic wars before she was born. *Jane Eyre* apparently begins just before the turn of the century, or so we would conclude from the reference to Sir Walter Scott's *Marmion* in Chapter 32. *Marmion*, published in 1808, is there described as "a new work," and Jane is about nineteen when St. John Rivers gives it to her. Thus the action of *Jane Eyre* takes place in the coaching era, before the advent of the railways. However, in certain respects it also reflects the economic and social changes of a little later period, as will be apparent in the next section.

SOCIAL CHANGES AND EDUCATION

Connected with the improvements in industry and transport was the rise of a new kind of ruling class, the mill-owners and mine-owners of the industrial age. As they gained in financial strength in their communities, they began to demand political power. The Reform Bill of 1832 (of which Charlotte, then a schoolgirl, wrote an enthusiastic account) gave this group the vote. They began to compete with the old landed gentry and went on in their turn to buy land, to build attractive houses, to travel, and to improve themselves generally. We see an old landed family and a member of the nouveau riche side by side in *Jane Eyre*, for while St. John Rivers is a member of an old family, it is Mr. Oliver, the taciturn needle manufacturer, who has the money. Notice that Oliver would be graciously willing to let his daughter marry into the Rivers family with its fine old traditions. Another example of a manufacturer of the new sort is Robert Moore in *Shirley*. The novel shows, among other things, the struggles of Moore to keep his mill going in the face of the opposition from workmen who have been thrown out of work by his new machines.

One of the ways in which the mill-owning families strove to improve themselves was by providing a good education for their children. In Yorkshire, as in other industrial areas, many families now had enough money to hire governesses and tutors for their children or to send them to school, if they so desired. At the same time there were many impoverished gentlewomen for whom being a governess was the one respectable career open to them. It was in this economic and social situation that girls of good background began to go out to work; and it was with this situation in mind that the Brontës made their plans for earning their living, which would one day be necessary if they were unmarried when their father died. All the girls were governesses in homes or schools, and Branwell was at one time a tutor. Eventually the girls planned to have a school of their own and so find security and independence. Two of the Brontë novels, *Jane Eyre* and Anne Brontë's *Agnes Grey*, concern the careers of governesses and give a good idea of their circumstances. Their position was indeed often an uncomfortable one, as Charlotte and Anne both felt. They were of a higher class than the servants and yet not on a level with the family, and in consequence the often suffered from loneliness and humiliation. They were also extremely poorly paid. Even later in the century, fifteen pounds a year, Jane's salary at Lowood, was a not uncommon sum; although it compared unfavorably with the pay received by miners and weavers, who usually earned between forty and sixty pounds a year. When she was a teacher in a boarding school, Charlotte herself wrote that when she had paid her expenses and bought clothes for herself and Anne, she had nothing left. Her heroine, Jane, was certainly one of the very poorest of wage earners.

RELIGIOUS BACKGROUND

The religious situation of the time is complex and ought to be understood, as a knowledge of it is assumed in *Jane Eyre* and other Brontë novels. The Church of England or Anglican Church (its American branch is called the Protestant Episcopal Church) was the Established Church of England; that is, it received financial support from the state and had essential ties with the Crown and Parliament. Reverend Patrick Brontë, the father of the Brontës, was an Anglican clergyman. Other Protestant bodies, which did not enjoy this connection with the state, were called "nonconformists" or "Dissenters." They included the Methodists, the Baptists, and the Congregationalists. Roman Catholics were a small minority at the time and were widely feared and disliked, partly because in the past they had often been suspected of alliance with England's Catholic enemies, Spain and France, and partly because they were thought to owe their first allegiance to the Pope rather than to the English Crown. Charlotte's letters from Belgium and her novel Villette, as well as Chapter 22 in *Jane Eyre*, attest to a prejudice against Catholicism which seems to the modern reader sheer bigotry; it should be remembered that her views were characteristic of the only society she knew.

During the eighteenth century, the Church of England was in a state of spiritual destitution. It was substantially controlled by the conservative landowning gentry, whose younger sons frequently held "livings" (positions) in the Church, lacked any real sense of vocation, and left their parish duties to their overworked subordinates. Large sections of the poorer classes, particularly in the new industrial areas, were out of touch with the Church altogether, and their widespread drunkenness and immorality seemed beyond the power of religion to redeem. Two related religious movements brought about some badly needed reformation in this state of affairs.

THE METHODIST REVIVAL

The brothers John and Charles Wesley, members of a society which undertook a "methodical" cultivation of the religious life, underwent deeply felt religious conversions before the middle of the eighteenth century. They devoted the rest of their lives to highly successful preaching missions to convert others to the new understanding they had attained. They believed that in Christ was forgiveness of sins and grace for a renewed life in His service. The new life would issue in joyous and spontaneous acts of piety and charity. Their preaching was immensely successful both in England and America and affected both the Church of England, of which they were ordained ministers, and the Methodist churches which their followers founded. Methodism was more emotional, appealed to large numbers of the deprived, uneducated population, and was, therefore, numerically strong. Within the Church of England, and persons affected by the religious revival were called "Evangelicals" and formed a relatively small but influential party. They wielded enormous moral power in their time and were behind such movements as the freeing of the slaves, the education of poor children, prison and factory reforms, and the distribution of pious literature to the working classes. They did much good, but, like every religion, Methodism and Evangelicalism were subject to perversion and their adherents to hypocrisy and fanaticism.

Although they were members of the Church of England, the Brontës were exposed to Methodist influence from both sides of the family. Mr. Brontë had once been connected with a Methodist school, and their Aunt Branwell, who brought them up, taught them Methodist hymns and prayers and lent them Methodist magazines. Moreover, Haworth had in the past been the scene of Methodist revivals. What was the effect on Emily and Charlotte Brontë of this exposure to Evangelical religion? To judge by the novels, their reaction seems to have been a negative one. In Wuthering Heights, we have the portrait of the grumbling, puritanical fanatic, Joseph; in *Jane Eyre* the meddling, loveless, hypocritical Mr. Brocklehust. Were those portraits drawn from life?

CHRONOLOGY OF THE BRONTËS

1812   Patrick and Maria Brontë married.

1813   Maria Brontë born.

1815   Elizabeth Brontë born.

1816   Charlotte Brontë born, April 21.

1817   Patrick Branwell Brontë born.

1818   Emily Jane Brontë born.

1820   Anne Brontë born.

1820   The Brontë family moves to Haworth.

1824   Maria, Elizabeth, Charlotte, and Emily Brontë sent to Cowan Bridge School.

1825   Maria and Elizabeth Brontë die.

1831–2   Charlotte at Roe Head.

1835–8   Charlotte at Roe Head as governess.

1842   Charlotte and Emily go to Brussels; Emily returns late that year, Charlotte in January 1844.

1846   Poems published.

1847   *Jane Eyre*, *Wuthering Heights*, *Agnes Grey* published.

1848   *Tenant of Wildfell Hall* published.

1848   Branwell and Emily die.

1849   Anne dies.

1849	*Shirley* published.
1852	*Villette* published.
1854	Charlotte and Arthur Bell Nicholls marry.
1855	Charlotte dies, March 31.
1857	Mrs. Gaskell's *Life of Charlotte Brontë* published.
1861	Mr. Brontë dies.
1906	Mr. Nicholls dies.

JANE EYRE

INTRODUCTION TO CHARLOTTE BRONTË LIFE OF CHARLOTTE BRONTË

The Brontës were one of the most extraordinary literary families who ever lived. They spent the greater part of their lives in an isolated Yorkshire village on the edge of the moors, not only cut off from the Victorian world of letters, but also to a large extent from the companionship of young people of their own age and education. Yet they became known and loved all over the world. Their books have been translated into many languages and are always high in reading popularity. Their home, Haworth Parsonage, is visited by Brontë lovers from many nations - by over 146,000 people in 1971. Every decade sees new attempts to dramatize their lives and works in plays or films. Finally, it has been estimated that there have been more items of critical writing on the Brontës than on any other English writer except Shakespeare. What is the source of the Brontë uniqueness and of their perennial appeal? We may seek the answer to this question in their unusual heredity and environment, in their own genius, in their effect on each other, and in the tragic nature of their lives.

Phyllis Bentley, herself a novelist and a Yorkshire-woman, has called attention to the favorable combination of Celtic heredity and Yorkshire environment in the Brontë temperament. Their parents were both Celtic, their mother being from Cornwall and their father from Ireland. Yet they grew up in Yorkshire and were in fact able to speak and write either an Irish brogue or a Yorkshire dialect with the greatest of ease. They thought of themselves as English, yet were aware of their Cornish and Irish descent. Miss Bentley comments: "The Yorkshire character (descended partially from Scandinavian elements) forms a great contrast to the Irish; it is vigorous, practical, prosaic, stubborn, broadly humorous and sparing of speech where the Irish is melancholy, passionate, proud, restless, eloquent, and witty. This striking contrast between the Brontës' heredity and their environment played, as we shall see, a highly important part in forming the nature of their work." (See her book *The Brontë Sisters*, p. 12.) [The Celts, for our present purpose, were the inhabitants of the British Isles pushed to the west and north of England by the Anglo-Saxons and Danish invaders.]

Next, all the young Brontës were talented and precocious. Now, of course, gifted children are not rare. But Charlotte, Branwell, Emily, and Anne Brontë were a rare combination. What is unique in the Brontë family is the spectacle of four gifted children, two of them (Charlotte and Emily) geniuses, growing up together, more or less isolated from other children and from the society around them, inventing stories and entertaining each other with them, creating for themselves and imaginary world, and living so completely in that word that it often seemed more real to them than the everyday doings around them. More will be said about this imaginary world presently.

Finally, it can be truthfully claimed that for all the Brontës life was in some sense tragic. Originally there were six of them.

The two older girls died within a few weeks of each other before they entered their teens. All the others died before they were forty. Anne and Emily, the youngest, died with books planned which they were never able to write. Branwell, the only boy, the delight and hope of his sisters, died with his promise completely unfulfilled, a drunkard and a drug addict. Charlotte lived to win the fame and independence they had all longed for; but when it came, she was too tired, too ill, too alone, and too grief-stricken to enjoy it.

HAWORTH PARSONAGE

But these sad days were in the future on a spring day in 1820 when the Reverend and Mrs. Patrick Brontë, their household goods in seven carts, mounted the steep hill to Haworth village. Their church towered above the village; higher still stood the parsonage which was to be their home, as long as any of them should live. Its front windows looked out on the graveyard and the church, but behind the house lay the moors-sombre, limitless, inviting.

Perhaps the six children also rode up in the carts. The two "big girls," Maria and Elizabeth, seven and five, would probably be expected to look after four-year-old Charlotte, and Branwell, who was not yet three. Emily and Anne were babies. Before long the older children were left much on their own, as their mother became very ill with cancer and could not bear to have them see her suffer. Someone overheard her repeating, "O God, my poor children; O God, my poor children." She died in the fall of 1821, and probably the younger children did not remember her. It is clear that Maria, an intelligent and loyal child, tried to take her place and mother her little sisters and brother. Mrs. Brontë's sister, Aunt Branwell, gave up her home in Cornwall to look after the children and the house. She brought up the girls to be efficient housekeepers and set them an example of courtesy and good breeding, but otherwise left them much to themselves.

The head of the household, the Reverend Patrick Brontë, seems to have been quite a complex character, and biographers have not always done him justice. There is a tendency to dwell on his eccentricities, such as his fear of fire (he allowed no drapes in the parsonage), his habit of firing a pistol out of a door or window, and his custom of eating alone. Eccentric he certainly was, but it is equally clear that he loved his children, talked with them as equals on subjects of interest to them all (usually politics), saw that they had plenty to read, bought them toys, and encouraged them to be as independent and courageous in their thinking as he was himself. Most of all, he respected their right to lives of their own: their secret games and plays were never interfered with. His greatest error was that he was not at all strict with Branwell, whom he kept at home and tutored himself; the whole family paid dearly for this. However, his daughters loved and respected him as long as they lived. He was immoderately proud of Charlotte's success and did all he could to guard her memory.

THE CLERGY DAUGHTERS' SCHOOL AT COWAN BRIDGE

But for the present the children had to be educated so that they could earn their living. Mr. Brontë, left with six small children to bring up, must have been relieved when he heard that a fellow-clergyman, the Reverend W. Carus Wilson, had founded the Clergy Daughters' School for the daughters of poor clergy. Here Maria and Elizabeth (now eleven and nine) were entered in the spring of 1824, and here Charlotte (eight) and Emily (barely six) followed them later in the same year.

The Clergy Daughters' School, located at Cowan Bridge near Kirkby Lonsdale made a deep and painful impression on Charlotte Brontë. She used her memories of her school days when she wrote the early chapters of *Jane Eyre*. The school was the original of Lowood, where the Reeds sent Jane after her illness; the "black marble clergyman," Mr. Brocklehurst, is based on Charlotte's impression of Mr. Carus Wilson, and Helen Burns, who dies in Chapter 9, is Maria Brontë as Charlotte remembered her. (Charlotte claimed over and over that her picture of Helen Burns was drawn from life and was if anything understated.) It is therefore important to understand something about the Reverend Carus Wilson and the school at Cowan Bridge.

Mr. Carus Wilson was a clergyman of the Church of England who had very early come under Evangelical influences (see Religious Background). He had a profound fear of hell and a hatred of sin; at one point at least he maintained that grievous sin after baptism cannot be forgiven. He also had a vivid faith in divine grace and in heavenly rewards for the righteous. Like other evangelicals he believed in and pursued works of charity. At the age of eight he distributed religious tracts, and while at college he openly rebuked some army officers for swearing. He founded low-priced religious periodicals, many copies of which can still be seen today in the British Museum in England. They contain hundreds of little stories about naughty boys and girls who meet sudden death and go to hell (see under Brocklehurst), or who make stupendous sacrifices and to go heaven.

The publication of these periodicals was not Mr. Carus Wilson's only charitable work. He also founded five schools, one of which was Cowan Bridge. There he planned to educate sixty or seventy poor clergymen's daughters. "In all cases," he wrote in his prospectus, "the great object in view is their intellectual and religious improvement; and to give them that plain and useful education which may best fit them to return with respectability and advantage to their own homes, or to maintain themselves in the different stations of life to which Providence may call them."

Many years later, long after *Jane Eyre* was published and after Charlotte herself was dead, Mr. Carus Wilson wrote as follows: "The pupils are necessarily put into a very simple and uniform attire. Many of them no doubt feel it. They have been unfortunately accustomed perhaps even to excess in this very prevailing and increasing love of dress; for alas! clergymen's families are not exempt from the mania, - not even the poorest. With me it was always an object to nip in the bud any growing symptoms of vanity ... And let me add, that I am sure the more that trivial and useless work is discountenanced amongst the pupils, the better. My dearest desire is that they should be brought up usefully, not tawdrily. The tinsel and varnish are of little moment compared with excellence in plain useful work. It will be a sorry look-out for a clergyman's daughter, if she is sent out from the school, for instance, a first-rate performer in crotchet and worsted work, and that sort of thing - however useful this may be - but unable to cut out, and make, and mend her own garments." [Taken from Carus Wilson's *Thoughts Suggested to the Superintendent and Ladies of the Clergy Daughters' School*, Ventnor: T. Butler, 1858, pp. 39–40.]

Such was the school to which the four Brontë girls were sent in 1824. The site was low, damp, and unhealthy, the food unappetizing, and the rules very strict for children accustomed to affection and freedom. Maria seems to have suffered the most. Judging by Charlotte's account of Helen Burns, she was a sweet, intelligent, and thoughtful child, but absent-minded and careless - the very type to irritate a strict disciplinarian as Helen irritated Miss Scatcherd in *Jane Eyre*. Maria and Elizabeth had recently had whooping cough when they entered the school and never seem to have been strong. They went into what was then called a "decline" - probably tuberculosis. Maria was sent home very ill and died in May, 1825; Elizabeth followed her and died in June of that year. Charlotte was convinced to the end of her days that the conditions at Cowan Bridge had killed her sisters. She took her revenge in *Jane Eyre*. At this late date it is hard to say whether or not this was a fair judgment. Certainly the conditions at the school were not good and equally certainly many parents were alarmed at the amount of illness in the school, for twenty-eight out of seventy-seven children were taken out of the school that spring (1825). Among them were Charlotte and Emily Brontë.

For the second time the Brontë children had lost a mother, for Maria had tried to be a mother to them. Now this role fell to Charlotte, aged nine. From that time on she tried to guide and help and protect her brother and her sisters.

THE SECRET DREAM WORLD

For five and a half years Mr. Brontë did not send any of the children away to school. They were taught at home and were looked after by their aunt, Miss Branwell and by a new servant, Tabitha Ackroyd, a warmhearted, independent, outspoken Yorkshirewoman who did the rough work of the house and entertained the children with folk tales and ballads. Tabby, as she was called, was with them practically all their lives and died at eighty-five, a month before Charlotte. Some characteristics of Bessie Lee and Hannah (Chap. 28 on) in *Jane Eyre* and of Nelly Dean in *Wuthering Heights* are based in part on the girls' recollections of Tabby.

Once the children's chores and lessons were done, they were free to read or play as they pleased. There were plenty of books in the parsonage, and the children read these and all the magazines and newspapers which the adults subscribed to. Because of their father's enthusiasm, they took a great interest in politics and in recent history. The Duke of Wellington, who defeated Napoleon Bonaparte at Waterloo, was a great favorite. Their powerful imaginations added strange and marvelous fantasies to the facts they heard or read. They soon began to invent their own stories or "plays," as they called them. We know from Charlotte's own account that the first "play," called the "Young Men," was started in 1826 when she was ten. She wrote: "Papa bought Branwell some wooden soldiers at Leeds; when Papa came home it was night, and we were in bed, so next morning Branwell came to our door with a box of soldiers. Emily and I jumped out of bed, and I snatched up one and exclaimed, 'This is the Duke of Wellington! This shall be Duke!' When I had said this Emily likewise took one up and said it should be hers; when Anne came down, she said one should be hers. Mine was the prettiest of the whole, and the tallest, and the most perfect in every part. Emily's was a grave-looking fellow, and we called him 'Gravey.' Anne's was a queer little thing, much like herself, and we called him 'Waiting boy.' Branwell chose his, and called him 'Bonaparte.'"

The children sent the Twelve, as they called them, to Africa, made Wellington king of a new realm, and built him a capital city which they called Great Glass Town. Gradually they created an entire new world with its own wars, politics, high society, literature, and art. The children wrote accounts of the romances, battles, debates, and other events of their imaginary kingdom. They even "published" *The Young Men's Magazine*, which imitated the grown-up magazines they read, except that their issues were very tiny-proportioned perhaps to the size of the wooden "Twelve." Some were only an inch and a half long. About a hundred of these minute booklets, printed in tiny script and carefully bound in blue or grey paper cut from sugar-wrappers, are still in existence today at the Parsonage Museum in Haworth, at the University of Texas, and at other great libraries.

There were other "plays": "Our Fellows," begun in 1828, and "The Islanders," begun in 1829. Charlotte gives a charming account of the origin of the latter: "The play of *The Islanders* was formed in December, 1827, in the following manner. One night, about the time when the cold sleet and fogs of November are succeeded by the snowstorms, and high piercing night-winds of confirmed winter, we were all sitting around the warm blazing kitchen fire, having just concluded a quarrel with Tabby, concerning the propriety of lighting a candle, from which she came off victorious, no candle having been produced. A long pause succeeded, which was at last broken by Branwell saying, in a lazy manner, 'I don't know what to do.' This was echoed by Emily and Anne.

Tabby. 'What ya may go t' bed.'

Branwell. 'I'd rather do anything than that.'

Charlotte. 'Why are you so glum tonight, Tabby? Oh! suppose we had each an island of our own.'

Branwell. 'If we had I would choose the Island of Man.'

Charlotte. 'And I would choose the Isle of Wight.'

Emily. 'The Isle of Arran for me.'

Anne. 'And mine should be Guernsey.'

"We then chose who should be chief men in our islands. Branwell chose John Bull, Astley Cooper, and Leigh Hunt; Emily, Walter Scott, Mr. Lockhart, Johnny Lockhart; Anne, Michael

Sadler, Lord Bentinck, Sir Henry Halford. I chose the Duke of Wellington and two sons, Christopher North and Co., and Mr. Abernethy. Here our conversation was interrupted by the, to us, dismal sound of the clock striking seven, and we were summoned off to bed. The next day we added many others to our list of men, till we got almost all the chief men of the kingdom. After this, for a long time, nothing worth noticing occurred. In June, 1828, we erected a school on a fictitious island, which was to contain 1,000 children. The manner of the building was as follows. The Island was fifty miles in circumference, and certainly appeared more like the work of enchantment than anything real ..." [Here the MS. breaks off.] The "Chief Men" chosen by the children were all well-known men of the day. The children thought of themselves as the Genii who had power over the destinies of their creations. Charlotte called herself Talii, and the others Branii, Emmii, and Annii. They supplied their creations with a continuous set of adventures ranging over imaginary territories called Angria and Gondal and over three generations. Many children invent such fantastic sagas, but those invented by the Brontë children are unique in that they were joint creations of four exceptionally gifted children who wrote in close cooperation. They were unique in another way. The Brontës loved their world of fantasies so much that they continued to invent it and to live in it after they were grown up. In 1845, when Emily was twenty-seven and Anne twenty-five, they were still "playing" with their imaginary characters. Charlotte gave them up, evidently with grief, for she wrote a touching farewell to her old play-fellows when she was twenty-three. Branwell never really outgrew them.

The children have been well described: "Page after page of these little books flew from their busy hands, until the bedroom and dining-room of the parsonage were thick with records of Angria. The two children were to be seen at all hours, carefully folding and stitching the tiny sheets, their pens scratching out the printed characters that had to serve for type; Charlotte's head almost touching the paper, her short-sighted eyes closely following every letter; Branwell, tightly holding his nose between thumb and forefinger, speaking rapidly, and writing down the resultant sounds, which he had christened the Young Men's language. Day after day, month after month, year after year, they wrote on, their imaginations spilling out endlessly into the Angrian world. And when, their hands too tired to hold the pen, they walked over the moors to their secret waterfall, to some lonely farm in its fold of the hills, to the village shop for fresh supplies of papers ... they sauntered in a delightful dream, weaving fresh romances or bloody battles as they went; treading, not Yorkshire earth, but the hard, sun-baked soil of Angria; seeing, not a Haworth shepherd or mill hand, but gorgeously apparelled Angrian nobles and their ladies." (From Lawrence and E. M. Hanson, *The Four Brontës*, p. 20; for further reading on the Angria and Gondal sagas, see the relevant chapters in books listed in the bibliography. Fannie Ratchford's book, listed there, is the most detailed account.)

Charlotte wrote her best poem on the Angrian fantasies:

We wove a web in childhood, A web of sunny air; We dug a spring in infancy Of water pure and fair; We sowed in youth a mustard seed, We cut an almond rod; We are now grown up to riper age: Are they withered in the sod? Are they blighted, failed and faded Are they moldered back to clay? For life is darkly shaded, And its joys fleet fast away!

HOME AND SCHOOL 1831-1835

The hours they spent in their kingdoms, Angria and Gondal, were probably the happiest in the Brontës' lives. But it was necessary to think seriously of more formal education. If Mr. Brontë died, the girls would have no home and no one to look after them. The one profession open to a genteel young woman of little means was to be a governess (see Introduction). To get more education for this purpose, Charlotte was sent to Miss Wooler's school at Roe Head near Huddersfield. She remained there for eighteen months. Apart from the few months at Cowan Bridge, this was the total period of Charlotte's formal education until she went to Brussels ten years later. She worked tremendously hard to learn all she could, so that she would be able to teach Emily and Anne when she returned. For the first time she made friends outside her own family, Mary Taylor and Ellen Nussey, both of whom remained her close friends for the rest of her life. Both have left their impressions of her when at fifteen she arrived at Roe Head. Mary said she looked like a little old woman in her worn, unfashionable dress. She was so shortsighted that she always seemed to be peering at something, moving her head from side to side to see it. The other girls thought she was funny because she did not like games, did not know any grammar or geography, and spoke with a strong Irish accent. She knew a great deal of poetry by heart. Mary remembered telling Charlotte she was ugly. Ellen agreed that she was "anything but pretty ... Her naturally beautiful hair of soft silky brown being then dry and fuzzy-looking, screwed up in tight little curls, showing features that were all the plainer from her exceeding thinness and want of complexion." She first discovered Charlotte, who was very homesick and who missed the Angrian game, crying in a large bay window. Like Mary, Ellen remarked on Charlotte's ignorance of the usual elementary subjects contrasted with her wide knowledge of politics and literature.

Charlotte soon became known among the other girls for her ability as a storyteller, and one night, according to Ellen, she succeeded in frightening herself as well as the others: "Charlotte [once] caused ... a panic of terror by her thrilling relations of the wanderings of a somnambulist. She brought together all the horrors her imagination could create, from surging seas, raging breakers, towering castle walls, high precipices, invisible chasms and dangers. Having wrought these materials to the highest pitch of effect, she brought out, in almost cloud-height, her somnambulist, walking on shaking turrets, - all told in a voice that conveyed more than words alone can express. A shivering terror seized the recovered invalid; a pause ensued; then a subdued cry of pain came from Charlotte herself, with a terrified command to others to call for help. She was in bitter distress. Something like remorse seemed to linger in her mind after this incident; for weeks there was no prevailing upon her to resume her tales, and she never again created terrors for her listeners."

To readers of *Jane Eyre*, it is interesting that at fifteen Charlotte was still grieving for her dead sisters. Both Mary and Ellen record this. Mary said Charlotte spoke of Maria and Elizabeth as "wonders of talent and kindness." She even dreamed about them. Ellen said Charlotte talked a great deal about them. "Her love for them was most intense; a kind of adoration dwelt in her feelings which, as she conversed, almost imparted itself to her listener. She described Maria as a little mother among the rest, superhuman in goodness and cleverness. But the most touching of all were the revelations of her sufferings, - how she suffered with the sensibility of a grown-up person, and endured with patience and fortitude that were Christ-like. Charlotte would still weep and suffer when thinking of her." Charlotte's grief should be borne in mind when studying the description of Helen Burns in *Jane Eyre*.

From July 1832 to July 1835, Charlotte taught her sisters at home. Besides this, Emily and Anne had piano lessons (Charlotte was too near-sighted), and all four children had drawing lessons.

Branwell was supposedly preparing to study art at the Royal Academy of Art, but he already had too much leisure time and too little suitable companionship. All four continued to write their Angrian and Gondal tales - secretly. Charlotte apparently never told anyone but Mary Taylor of these writings, and she refused to show the little books even to her.

NEW UNDERTAKINGS 1835-1841

In 1835 the four young people began to go their separate ways. Charlotte went back to Roe Head to teach, Emily accompanying her as a pupil. After two months of homesickness, she became ill and was replaced by Anne. However, Emily soon had to leave home again to teach at a school near Halifax where, according to one account, she told her pupils she liked dogs better than little girls! Branwell mysteriously abandoned his plans to go to the Royal Academy. Charlotte worried a great deal about her family. She disliked teaching, missed writing her Angrian stories, and suffered from a kind of religious melancholia at this point. These anxieties affected her health, and she left Miss Wooller's School in May, 1838. However, all of the girls were obliged to go out and earn money. The following spring, Anne took a post for some months and two years later went as governess to a family named Robinson at Thorp Green, where she stayed for nearly five years. Charlotte held two posts during these years. She was not happy as a governess, since she had little knack for managing children, longed to be at her writing, and was miserable living in other peoples' houses. Emily also disliked being away from home and eventually returned to take over some of the housework from her aunt. Branwell had tried his hand at portrait-painting and failed, tried to get some of his writing published and failed, and was working as a railway clerk. The future did not look very bright for any of them.

BRUSSELS AND THE SCHOOL PLAN, 1841-1843

Since the future looked so dismal, Charlotte, who was usually the leader, took steps to better their position. Without immediate prospects of marriage, they had to earn money; they had to teach; they wanted to be together. What if they were to start their own school? But for that Charlotte knew they needed more education. She determined to get it and persuaded Aunt Branwell to finance them. Specifically, they needed French, a staple in young ladies' education in those days. The idea of Belgium rather than France seems to have come from Charlotte's friend Mary Taylor, who, with her sister Martha, was at school there. Charlotte wrote to Ellen; "I hardly know what swelled to my throat as I read her letter; such a vehement impatience of restraint and steady work; such a strong wish for wings - wings such as wealth can furnish; such an urgent thirst to see, to know, to learn; something internal seemed to expand bodily for a minute."

Eventually it was settled that she and Emily would go to the Pensionnat Heger in Brussels, a large school with about a hundred pupils, and there Mr. Brontë took them in February, 1842. Charlotte's stay there was to be of momentous significance in her life. Determined to get the most out of their precious time abroad, both girls worked extremely hard. They were fortunate in having a very gifted teacher in M. Heger, who recognized their ability and took great pains with their studies. He was a lively, quick-tempered, warmhearted little man, only seven years older than Charlotte. He excelled, according to another of his pupils, "in calling out one's best faculties; in stimulating one's natural gifts; in fastening one's attention on models of perfection; in inspiring one with a sense of reverence and love for them..." In the Brontës he had wonderful material, and they rose to his challenge - even the shy Emily, though she was quite ready in her independent way to argue with his methods. Charlotte adored it, "I returned to it [i.e., learning] with the same avidity that a cow, that has long been kept on dry hay, returns to fresh grass. Don't laugh at my **simile**. It is natural to me to submit." By fall both were given teaching responsibilities, Charlotte in English and Emily in music. Unfortunately, their schooling was interrupted late in October when Aunt Branwell died. They both returned to Haworth. Emily never returned to Brussels, although M. Heger wrote a charming letter to Mr. Brontë praising his daughters' ability and character and promising at least one of them a position when their studies were complete.

Charlotte did go back, after Christmas, for exactly another year. She became quite fluent in French and worked hard at German. However, she was not very happy. She missed Emily and did not find it easy to make friends with the Belgian girls. This was her own fault, since her letters show that she was intolerant of them because she thought them frivolous, superficial, Catholic, and foreign. (In some ways Charlotte was a true daughter of a provincial Victorian parson.) Martha Taylor had died, and Mary Taylor had left Brussels. Not only had she no longer her English friends but something had come between her and the Hegers. She explained that Madame Heger was cold and that she did not see much of Mr. Heger any more, though occasionally he gave her a book. She became very lonely, miserable, and homesick. Eventually she worked herself into the highly nervous emotional state which she describes so well in Villette, and astonishingly, in spite of her anti-Catholic sentiments, made a confession to a Catholic priest in the Cathedral of Ste. Gudule.

She describes this both in a letter to Emily and in Villette, but we do not know what she confessed. Another extraordinary fact about her state of mind is that she wrote Branwell that "... always in the evening when I am in the great dormitory alone, having no other company than a number of beds with white curtains, I always recur as fanatically as ever to the old ideas, the old faces, and the old scenes in the world below ... " - the Angrian world of their childhood imaginings.

Was there any reason for Charlotte's unhappiness other than homesickness and social isolation? Some biographers believe she was deeply in love with M. Heger; others deny it. There is little but circumstantial evidence. Charlotte certainly never says she loved her teacher, but then she would have been ashamed of an unrequited love in an impossible situation (see her remarks in *Jane Eyre*, Chapter 16). Her letters to M. Heger show deep emotion, but are expressed in language appropriate from a pupil to a master. Luck Snow in Villette again is much like Charlotte, and she is in love with M. Paul, who is certainly a portrait of M. Heger; but this is fiction. M. Heger's coldness, which Charlotte says made her both laugh and cry, can be explained on other grounds. Perhaps the most persuasive piece of evidence is a poem in which Charlotte speaks of her master as being deaf to her pleas.

He was mute as the grave, he stood stirless as a tower At last I looked up and saw I prayed to stone: I asked help of that which to help had no power, I sought love where love was utterly unknown.

But even this is not entirely conclusive. The reader is advised to read Charlotte's novels and letters and decide for himself. Biographers vary in their estimates of the depth and nature of Charlotte's feeling for M. Heger. That it deepened her experience of human nature and made her a better novelist is beyond all question.

Charlotte returned to Haworth in January, 1844. Now was the moment to start their school for which she had endured so much suffering. But Mr. Brontë's sight was so bad that the girls did not like to leave him. They tried for a time to attract pupils to Haworth itself, but without success. Moreover, as time went on, Branwell added to their problems. He had been dismissed for negligence from his post with the railway.

Anne got him a post as tutor in the same family (the Robinsons) which employed her. But he was dismissed by the Robinsons, under circumstances which remain obscure, in 1845. A daydreamer (in this respect he had never left Angria), Branwell was by now an alcoholic and an opium addict. His deterioration distressed his family, who had expected so much of him. Charlotte, who had been closest to him as a child, was particularly dismayed. His condition very soon made any thoughts of having a school in the parsonage quite impossible. Once again the position of the Brontë girls seemed hopeless.

THE "BELLS," 1845 TO 1847

But once again Charlotte refused to give up. She had no job; Anne had no job (she had to leave the Robinsons); Emily was still at home, without work; Mr. Brontë's eyes were failing; Branwell was degenerating daily. So far all Charlotte's plans had failed. But now she had a new one. They would write. "Accidentally," one day, she had come across some of Emily's poems, and they had given her new hope. "I know that no woman that ever loved ever wrote such poetry before ... wild, melancholy, elevating." Emily was very angry at the invasion of her privacy, but eventually she and Anne were both won over to Charlotte's conviction that they ought to publish their poems. This they were obliged to do at their own expense - some of Aunt Branwell's little legacy went for this - and the book appeared in May, 1846. As women writers were sometimes not taken seriously, the Brontë girls chose as pseudonyms Currer, Ellis, and Acton Bell. The Poems sold only two copies, but having made one effort, the Brontës were already embarked on another. Each of them was writing a novel: Charlotte, *The Professor* (based in part on her Brussels experience); Anne, *Agnes Grey*; and Emily *Wuthering Heights*. Charlotte was not able to sell *The Professor*, but eventually it was arranged that *Agnes Grey* and *Wuthering Heights* would be published as one three-volume set by T. C. Newby. Meanwhile Mr. Brontë's cataract condition had become very serious, and his daughters were obliged to override his objections to an operation. They arranged to have this done in Manchester, where Charlotte took him to a physician in August, 1846. By his wish she stayed in the room while the operation was performed. For some weeks Mr. Brontë had to be kept very quiet in a darkened room until the bandages were removed and he could see again. Charlotte, despite her anxiety and a severe toothache, occupied herself by starting another novel. It was called *Jane Eyre* and about a year later was bought for five hundred pounds by Messrs. Smith, Elder and Company. Published in October, it went into a second edition in December, and in the main got very enthusiastic reviews. "Currer Bell" was famous. At last Charlotte was a success. However, she was very eager to keep her identity a secret. For one thing, privacy mattered to all of them, especially to Emily who was exceptionally reserved. For another, Charlotte had drawn some of her characters from life and naturally wanted to continue to do so. However, the mysterious Bells aroused great curiosity and there was much speculation as to who they were and whether they were men or women. Charlotte made matters worse by dedicating the second edition of *Jane Eyre* to the novelist William Thackeray (see her preface to the second edition) and found out only after it was in print that Thackeray himself had an insane wife. This made some people think that Thackeray or someone who knew his plight had written the novel. Finally, Emily's publisher T. C.

Newby woke up and realized that there was a market for Bell books. He accepted Anne's second book, *The Tenant of Wildfell Hall*, and told its American publisher that it was by the author of *Jane Eyre*. Meanwhile, Smith, Elder and Co. had promised the same American publisher, at a price, the sheets of Currer Bell's next book. Indignant at what seemed to be some kind of crookedness, the American wrote Smith, Elder, demanding an explanation. Smith, Elder (in the person of young Mr. George Smith) immediately wrote a puzzled query to Mr. Currer Bell at Haworth.

We can imagine the consternation at the parsonage. Charlotte was horror-stricken. Her publishers must think the Bells guilty of dishonesty and double-dealing. Her honor and Anne's were at stake. There was only one thing to be done. Shy as they were, they caught the first train they could, travelled all night, and appeared the next day in the office of the astonished George Smith, to show him that there were at least two Bells! Mr. Smith, once he got over his astonishment, rallied his resources, introduced them to his colleague William Smith Williams, invited them to dinner, took them to the opera, the Royal Academy, and the National Gallery, and sent them home several days later loaded with books. What a lot they must have had to tell the family!

DEATH AND SOLITUDE 1848-1852

It is sad to think how brief the Brontë triumph was. By 1848 Charlotte had achieved her mission. She and her sisters could look forward to financial security, to more writing, to publication. She herself was already as famous as she could wish to be and could - and did - correspond with some of the most noted literary people of the day. Yet within a year of their first triumph, she had already suffered losses in her family circle. "When I saw you and Mr. Smith in London," Charlotte wrote to William Smith Williams, "I little thought of all that was to come between July and Spring, how my thoughts were to be carried away from imagination, enlisted and absorbed in realities the most cruel."

Branwell was the first to die. For too long he had spent his days stupefied by liquor or opium. At night his father looked after him as best he could. "The poor old man and I have had a terrible night of it," Branwell would say. If Charlotte's letters are an indication, his sisters do not seem to have realized how seriously ill he was. Even the doctor did not expect his death. According to one report, his old friend, the sexton, John Brown, noticed the change in him and called the family. Charlotte remarked that religious feeling, long absent, and "a return of natural affection marked his last moments." Having hardened her heart toward Branwell in those last months, she suffered intensely when he died. "All his vices were and are nothing now We remember only his woes," she wrote, and in another letter, "He is in God's hands now; and the All-Powerful is likewise the All-Merciful."

Emily was stricken next. It is said that she caught cold at Branwell's funeral and never went out of the parsonage again. Charlotte's letters remark on the pain in her sister's chest, the shortness in her breathing, her pallor, and her emaciated appearance. "She is a real stoic in illness. She neither seeks nor will accept sympathy. To put any questions, to offer any aid, is to annoy; she will not yield a step before pain or sickness." The progress of tuberculosis was swift. "Never in all her life had she lingered over any task … and she did not linger now. She sank rapidly. She made haste to leave us. Day by day, when I saw with what a front she met suffering, I looked on her with an anguish of wonder and love. I have seen nothing like it; but, indeed, I have never seen her parallel in anything. Stronger than a man, simpler than a child, her nature stood alone. The awful point was that, while full of truth for others, on herself she had no pity; the spirit was inexorable to the flesh; from the trembling hands, the unnerved limbs, the fading eyes, the same service was exacted as they had rendered in health. To stand by and witness this, and not dare to remonstrate, was a pain no words can render." Emily died on the horsehair sofa in the living room about two o'clock in the afternoon, December 19, 1848. She was just thirty years old. Charlotte wrote "We are very calm at present ... The anguish of seeing her suffer is over; the spectacle of the pains of death is gone by; the funeral is past. We feel she is at peace. No need to tremble now for the hard frost and keen wind. Emily does not feel them."

Anne, already ill before Emily died, soon became worse. Three weeks after Emily's death a doctor from Leeds pronounced her already in serious condition. Like Emily, she had tuberculosis. She was more patient than Emily, more ready to receive help, more ready to hope. Her great desire, as the disease progressed, was to see the sea again at Scarborough. She felt if she could only breathe sea air once more, she might recover. After many delays Charlotte and Ellen Nussey went with her to Scarborough in May, 1849. Anne pointed out to her sister and friend the beauties of the Yorkshire landscape, drove a donkey cart on the beach, watched a glorious sunset, and died the next day early in the afternoon, about the same time as Emily. Her last words were, "Take courage, Charlotte, take courage."

Indeed, Charlotte needed extraordinary courage at this point. Within a few months she had lost all her contemporaries in her family. After burying Anne at Scarborough (where her grave, bright with flowers, can still be seen), she returned to

Haworth. "All was clear and bright, waiting for me," she wrote Ellen. "Papa and the servants were well ... The dogs seemed in a strange ecstasy. I am certain they regarded me as a harbinger of others ... I shut the door - I tried to be glad that I came home ... I felt that the house was all silent - The rooms were all empty ... The agony that was to be undergone, and was not to be avoided came on. I underwent it ..."

With great courage and determination, Charlotte pursued the path she had set for herself. She ran the house and tried to cheer her father. She went on with Shirley, which she had started before Branwell died. (It was published late in 1849.) She revised and edited her sisters' works for publication. She visited London from time to time, where she met her literary idol, Thackeray, the writer Harriet Martineau, the critic G. H. Lewes, and other well-known people. She went to Edinburgh and to the Lake District, where she was introduced to a fellow-novelist Mrs. Gaskell, who later wrote her official biography. But Charlotte was often very lonely. "Sometimes when I wake in the morning," she wrote Ellen, "and know that Solitude, Remembrance, and Longing are to be almost my sole companions all day - That at night I shall go to bed with them, that they will long keep me sleepless - That next morning I shall wake to them again, - sometimes, Nell, I have a heavy heart of it." But she went on, "but crushed I am not, yet; nor robbed of elasticity, nor of hope, nor quite of endeavor." She kept up a large correspondence and did a great deal of reading - for her kind publishers kept her regularly supplied with the latest books. Her letters of the time (see the bibliography under Wise) make fascinating reading. She also visited Mrs. Gaskell and Miss Martineau when she came to know them better. Though she was troubled by illness and terrible depression, she went on with her daily tasks and tried to keep cheerful for her father's sake. It was in this period, toward the end of 1849, that "Currer Bell" was publicly identified with Charlotte Brontë. The secret, which had for a long time been kept even from Ellen Nussey, was finally out. After the first shock, Charlotte enjoyed the enthusiasm with which the local people read her books.

It was some time, though, before she summoned up the energy to complete her fourth and, as it turned out, last novel, Villette. Based on her experiences in Brussels, it proved painful to write; and there were days and weeks when she did not progress at all and worried for fear her publishers would be angry or because she knew her work would not have a social message! Her anxiety for her ailing father and her grief for her dead sisters were always present. Villette was finally published in December, 1852. It is a powerful and fascinating book, but a bitter and unhappy one. Fortunately, the reviews were on the whole very good, except that Harriet Martineau did not like the novel's emphasis on love. This criticism hurt Charlotte deeply. For her, love was the most important thing on earth, and whoever attacked love attacked the very heart of her world. "I know what love is, as I understand it," she wrote to Miss Martineau, "and if a man or woman should be ashamed of feeling love then there is nothing right, whole, faithful, truthful, unselfish in this world ..." This incident ended the friendship between them.

ARTHUR BELL NICHOLLS, 1852–1855

Meanwhile, Charlotte herself had been offered love from a very unexpected quarter. Arthur Bell Nicholls, a shy, rather stiff young Irishman, had been her father's curate (assistant) since 1844. Charlotte, who used him as the model for Mr. Macarthey in Shirley, thought him respectable and conscientious but narrow-minded and rather uninteresting. She was more embarrassed than pleased when in December, 1852, he proposed to her. "He stopped in the parsonage; he tapped; like lightning it flashed on me what was coming. He entered; he stood before me. What his words were you can guess; his manner you can hardly realize, nor can I forget it. Shaking from head to foot, looking deadly pale, speaking low, vehemently, yet with difficulty, he made me for the first time feel what it costs a man to declare affection where he doubts response." Mr. Brontë's reaction was violent. He did not intend that his famous daughter should marry a poor nobody. He treated Mr. Nicholls with anger and contempt. In the face of Mr. Brontë's hostility and Charlotte's refusal, Mr. Nicholls suffered in silence. After some time, Charlotte began to feel somewhat sorry for him. "Dear Nell,' she wrote, "without loving him, I don't like to think of him suffering in solitude and wish him anywhere so that he were happier."

One Sunday she went to the altar rail to receive Communion and her presence was too much for Mr. Nicholls. "He struggled, faltered, then lost command over himself-stood before my eyes and in the sight of the Communicants white, shaking, voiceless ... he made a great effort, but could only with difficulty whisper and falter through the service." He left Haworth for another position later that week, "trembling and miserable." Charlotte was already of two minds about him; one sentence in a letter to Ellen shows: "I may be losing the purest gem, and to me for the most precious life can give-genuine attachment - or I may be escaping the yoke of a morose temper."

Gradually the depth of Mr. Nicholls' feelings impressed her. They corresponded, at first secretly, then openly. Finally Mr. Brontë was persuaded into allowing Mr. Nicholls to call on Charlotte so that they might get to know each other better. Slowly her doubt and her father's hostility diminished. Finally, after many delays and many understandable doubts on Charlotte's part, they were married in June, 1854. Only Ellen and Miss Wooler were present. Charlotte's old teacher gave her away, as Mr. Brontë did not feel like coming.

The letters Charlotte wrote on her wedding trip to Ireland and during the next few months show that she was happier than she had dared to hope. She had not married a Mr. Rochester, but a perfectly ordinary, unimpressive, untalented man. (For a portrait of him as Charlotte saw him first, see Macarthey in *Shirley*, Chap. 37.) His religious outlook was even more narrowly Protestant than Charlotte's, and he did not share her interest in literature. Yet he made her happy, for he was kind and considerate, very serious about his work, and good to Mr. Brontë. Charlotte had never felt better or more contented. Even her nervous headaches disappeared. "My life is different from what it used to be," she wrote Ellen, "may God make me thankful for it. I have a good, kind, attached husband; and every day my attachment grows stronger." "My dear boy," she calls him in another letter, "certainly dearer now than he was six months ago." One source of satisfaction to Charlotte was that her father's parish would be taken care of in his last years. "Papa has taken no duty since we returned; and each time I see Mr. Nicholls put on gown and surplice, I feel comforted to think that this marriage has secured Papa good aids in his old age."

Once more Charlotte's happiness was short-lived. She caught cold on a walk to the waterfall one November day in 1854 and soon was ill of tuberculosis, the same disease which had killed so many of her family. She became rapidly worse and could not even be cheered by the news that a baby was on the way. Her pregnancy probably made her general condition worse, for she suffered a great deal from nausea and sickness. One of her last letters to Ellen read in part, "I find in my husband the tenderest nurse, the kindest support, the best earthly comfort that ever a woman had. His patience never fails, and it is lived by sad days and broken nights ... May God comfort and help you!" She died March 31, 1855. Mrs. Gaskell records that when she heard her husband praying for her, she said, "Oh, I am not going to die, am I? He will not separate us; we have been so happy."

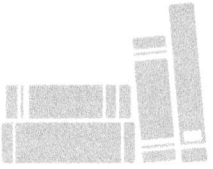

JANE EYRE

BACKGROUND

Charlotte Brontë's personal vision transformed everything she saw and experienced. For this reason it is not necessary or even possible to give a detailed account of her sources. However, some idea of the literary background of *Jane Eyre* may be useful. Novels about young girls who went out alone into the world, suffered various trials, miseries, and temptations, and emerged chaste and triumphant had been popular in England for over a century. One thinks, for example, of Richardson's Pamela and Fanny Burney's delightful Evelina, and there were scores of others. Another type of novel which had been very popular in the previous century was the Gothic romance which aimed at giving its readers a sensation of pleasant horror - horror based on fear of physical injury or fear of the supernatural. The settings of these novels were usually medieval castles or mosscovered ruins, with towering battlements, secret passageways, dismal dungeons, instruments of torture, ghostly visitations, ghostly music and voices, and ancient drapes and tapestries behind which lurked one knew not what. Charlotte's Angrian stories, the descriptions of the third floor at Thornfield, and the atmosphere of mystery and suspense certainly owe something to this tradition, which Charlotte may have encountered in Horace Walpole's *Castle of*

Otranto and Mrs. Radcliffe's *Mysteries of Udolpho*. In Charlotte's own time Sheridan Le Fanu was still writing tales of mystery and horror, and his *Chapters in the Life of a Tyrone Family* (1839), which concerned a bigamist whose blind wife tries to frighten the girl who has taken her place, and Carmilla in which he told a story of a vampire, may have provided hints for the Bertha Mason **episodes** in *Jane Eyre*. Charlotte's own favorite novelist was Sir Walter Scott, whose romances provided models for some of the Angrian stories (see Life). However, unless Charlotte took some hints from Staunton in *Heart of Midlothian* for her Byronic hero, or unless some of the "battlement" touches at Thornfield (the houses on which Charlotte based her descriptions did not have a third story) were from him, Scott's influence on *Jane Eyre* is confined to the scene where Bertha Mason appears on the roof, her hair streaming against the flames. Readers of Ivanhoe will remember Ulrica the Saxon hag similarly appearing on the flaming battlements shouting her vengeance-cry before falling to her death. The scene evidently made an unforgettable impression on Charlotte.

Scott was not the only Romantic writer who influenced Charlotte. In many respects she was a true heir to the Romantics poets, and what they accomplished through their poetry, she essays in her novel. *Jane Eyre* is infused with Romantic spirit: the longing for adventure, the insistence on liberty and independence, the emphasis on the rights of the individual soul to self-fulfillment, the love of the uncanny and the mysterious, and the intense sensibility to the changing face of nature all find expression in Charlotte's novel.

Two poets in particular influenced Charlotte - Byron and Wordsworth. The young Brontës read Byron, and Charlotte wrote imitations of his "Destruction of Sennacherib" (the model for her poem on the destruction of Great Glass Town) and his

"Hebrew Melodies." Moreover, Byron's poetic and public image as depicted in, for example, Childe Harold, Manfred, and Cain, captured her imagination and formed her taste in heroes. The typical Byronic hero is self-consciously melancholy, set apart from other men, a rebel and defier of orthodoxy. Though in the past he has committed many excesses and has become satiated in his experience of debauchery, he still glimpses an ideal of purity, which may or may not be attainable. He feels an outcast, damned by man and God, driven into exile. "Satanic" in his perversity, he has some of the vigor and independence of Milton's *Satan*. It is on this tradition that Charlotte drew in creating the Angrian Duke of Zamorna, the Marquis of Douro, and, to a degree, Mr. Rochester.

Less striking, but almost as pervasive, is the influence of Wordsworth. It is possible that his "Guilt and Sorrow," a narrative poem about a poor girl wandering destitute over Salisbury Plain, gave Charlotte some hints for Jane's desperate wandering and begging all around the village of Morton. His conviction that "Nature never did betray/the heart that loved her," that nature was a kind mother and loving teacher, underlies Chapter 28 of *Jane Eyre*, when Jane seeks repose on the open heath. She thinks of Nature as the "universal mother, Nature," who seems to her benign and good; "I thought she loved me, outcast as I was." Under the cloudless, awesome night sky, Jane is convinced of the immanence of God in Nature. "God is everywhere; but certainly we feel His presence most when His works are on the grandest scale spread before us." In her delight in the beauty of the countryside as the seasons pass, Charlotte displays a sensibility to the everyday details in nature which is akin to Wordsworth's own. Her heroine finds pleasure in the hungry robin perched in the leafless cherry-tree (Chap. 4), the snowdrops, crocuses, and pansies of spring, the "bright beck [stream], full of dark stones and sparkling eddies" (Chap. 9), the haymakers returning home in the summer dusk (Chap. 22), the great moth and the nightingale in the Thornfield orchard (Chap. 23), the sheep and the "mossy-faced lambs" on the swelling sweep of the moors above Morton (Chap. 30), a "hidden and lovely spot" near Ferndean where a dry stump provides a seat for the reunited lovers (Chap. 37). Charlotte's acute awareness of nature and her feeling of nearness to it - "I touched the heath: it was dry, yet warm with the heat of the summer day" (Chap. 28) - add to the haunting sense of the mystery and beauty of everyday life which infuses the book.

There had been several governess heroines before Jane, notably in Lady Blessington's *The Governess* and Harriet Martineau's *Deerbrook*. Then there was Becky Sharp in Thackeray's *Vanity Fair*, which was coming out in serial form just as *Jane Eyre* was published. Both Thackeray and Charlotte Brontë, however, broke with tradition in not making their governesses beautiful. Becky is pale and ginger-haired and Jane small and plain. Also, both are in different ways rebels against what society expects of them, whereas earlier governesses had generally been resigned and pathetic (as Anne's *Agnes Grey* was). It is Jane's rebelliousness, her dislike of servility, her insistence on equality with her master, and her claim that she had a right to feelings and passions which gives the book its uniqueness and force - and which shocked many of its early readers. In our society today the equality of women with men is held at least as a theoretical principle; and Charlotte's novel is one of the reasons why. (See especially Chaps. 12 and 23.)

Finally, Charlotte was influenced by her own earlier writings; like many other authors, she plagiarized her own works. Miss Fannie Ratchford, who studied the Angrian tales of the Brontë children, found that Charlotte had already experimented with some of the characters, themes, and episodes, which she used in *Jane Eyre*. She found, for example, an anticipation of Celine Varens, the French dancer, of a neglected charity child like Helen Burns, of a mother who spoiled her three children as did Mr. Reed, of a frivolous haughty blond like Georgiana Reed (actually named Georgiana), and of a handsome and powerful mad wife like Bertha Mason. In one of Charlotte's adolescent stories a heroine is actually in the charge of a grim hag rather as Bertha is in Grace Poole's charge and as Rebecca in Ivanhoe is in Ulrica's. The most impressive anticipation of *Jane Eyre* are the Byronic heroes of the Angrian fantasies, such as the Duke of Zamorna and the Marquis of Douro, who show many of the qualities later given to Rochester. Though not everyone would agree with Miss Ratchford that *Jane Eyre* "in its separate essential parts was complete before she bade farewell to Angria in 1839 or 1840," The Brontës' Web of Childhood should certainly be read for its fascinating account of Charlotte's early taste in fiction and her development as a writer.

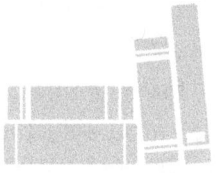

JANE EYRE

IMPORTANT FEATURES

1. The Angrian stories were fantastic, unrealistic, and romantic. Charlotte's first novel, The Professor, was determinedly prosaic, realistic, and unromantic. The two moods are combined in *Jane Eyre*. The novel is realistic in that its heroine is a humble governess, its other characters are mostly ordinary people, and its scenes are largely those of everyday life. But Charlotte infused her story with a romantic glow which transformed it and gave it some of the color, warmth, and excitement of Angria. This "Romanticized **Realism**" gives *Jane Eyre* its peculiar charm.

2. This mixture of moods may have affected the Style of the book, which is uneven in quality. At its best Charlotte's style is vigorous, supple, and straight-forward. Her ability to describe the simple things of nature, the changing seasons, the fire-lit interior, the intense emotions of the human heart, is hard to match. Yet from time to time she is guilty of wordiness and bombast; for example (in Chap. 15), various emotions in Rochester

"seemed momentarily to hold a quivering conflict in the large pupil dilating under his ebon eyebrows"; or again he is "fulminating strange anathemas." Sometimes, too, her ear for dialogue, so sound in the school scenes or in catching the dialect of Tabby, seems to fail her, especially in characters such as Rochester or Lady Blanche, who were creatures of her imagination and whose counterparts she did not know in actual life. Some of Blanche's speeches (in Chap. 17, for example) seem absurd. Charlotte's occasional failures in taste are probably due to her deficiency in the sense of the absurd. Yet she does not entirely lack a sense of humour. Some of the scenes between Jane and Rochester are delightful. But humour is not her strong point, and the sparkling wit, the balanced phrasing of Jane Austen's dialogue were not within her capabilities.

3. The Plot of *Jane Eyre* - plot in the sense of the external events - is, as Cecil says (p. 107) a "roaring melodrama," full of improbabilities and unlikely happenings. We should be very critical of such a plot if it appeared in a novel today. Yet somehow its melodramatic absurdities do not really bother us very much. Charlotte's very artlessness, her naivete in treating such a story of incredible happenings, carries us along with her; "her ingenuousness is an ingredient in her unique flavor ... it disinfects her imagination; blows away the smoke and sulphur which its ardent heat might be expected to generate, so that its flame burns pure and clear." - Cecil, p. 124. In defense of Charlotte, though, it is interesting to know that when she was a schoolgirl at Roe Head a squire in the region hid his mad wife and married a youthful governess.

4. It must be admitted that, in any case, these melodramatic happenings make an exciting story. Long practice in entertaining her brother, her sisters, and her schoolfellows had made Charlotte a mistress of the art of Suspense. Like her sister Emily, she constantly mystifies the reader by some puzzling or startling happening which is not immediately explained. His curiosity is constantly aroused. Why is Jane wanted in the breakfast room? Is it possible that the phlegmatic Grace Poole is really responsible for the mysterious laugh? Who is the stranger Mason, and why does his coming disturb Mr. Rochester? What can Mason mean when he says "she sucked the blood: she said she'd drain my heart"? Why does Rochester mutter "it will atone" in the midst of proposing marriage to Jane? Why do two strangers lurk in the churchyard on the morning of Jane's wedding? Why does St. John Rivers tear a scrap from one of Jane's papers? Where can Mr. Rochester be if Thornfield is deserted? One must read on. Charlotte's publisher, George Smith, one of the very first people ever to read *Jane Eyre*, started the book one weekend and cancelled all his engagements until he had finished it. Thousands of readers since must have read with the same abandon.

5. Charlotte excels, too, in suggesting the Mysterious and the Uncanny - usually without exactly invoking the supernatural. A good example is the atmosphere of strangeness and fear created in the red-room, where the terrified child Jane eventually faints from fright. Yet there is no real ghost or specter. The total effect is achieved by a number of suggestive details - the gloomy hangings and furniture, the chill, the silence, the solemnity of the room, the white little face in the mirror, the thought of Uncle Reed in the church vault, the fear that his spirit might rise

before her in the room, a sudden light gleaming on the walls. Such is their effect on us that we are not surprised when Jane hears the sound of rushing wings and screams out in terror. Even when Jane wakes up in her own bed, the horror has not quite dispersed, for the nursery fire looks like "a terrible red glare, crossed with thick black bars." A similar effect is created by the description of the third floor at Thornfield with its antique furniture and tapestries, its locked doors, its strange inhabitants, and the strange laugh, "distinct, formal, mirthless" which is sometimes heard in its halls. When the terrible cry rings through Thornfield in the dead of night, we are already prepared for something strange and dreadful. Similar touches add atmosphere to other episodes; examples are Jane's momentary fear of a Gytrash when Rochester first rides up with his dog (Chap. 12), the momentary appearance of the blood-red moon the night before her wedding, and her vision of her mother warning her to flee from temptation. Allied to these episodes, yet a little different, is the uncanny fact that when Rochester cries out for Jane, she hears his voice across the hills and he hears her answer. Even this Charlotte would probably not label supernatural or miraculous, but merely one example of the communication which can take place between souls who are somehow of the same substance - a circumstance which she assumes for Jane and Rochester as Emily assumes it for Cathy and Heathcliff.

6. She would probably argue that a similar mysterious interaction took place between man and Nature. At any rate, nature frequently provides her with appropriate settings for human emotion and action. The story of the orphan Jane opens on a chill November day when cold winds blow through leafless shrubs and rain pours on

the wet garden. At Lowood the wind whistles through the chinks in the bedrooms and freezes the girls as they walk to church - cold as the loveless charity the school typifies. Especially noteworthy are the pains Charlotte took with her settings for important encounters between Jane and Rochester. They meet on a clear, frosty night, as Jane from the stile watches the moonrise. On that same stile Mr. Rochester is sitting on a summer evening with the smell of hay and roses in the air when Jane returns from Gateshead. Sometimes they repair to the orchard, as after the strange night Jane spent with the wounded Mason. It is here, in an "Eden-like" nook that Rochester proposes to Jane on midsummer eve. Their reunion, in a more muted mood, takes place on an evening of "sad sky, cold gale and ... rain," in the wood-encircled manor of Ferndean.

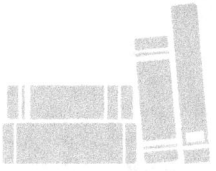

JANE EYRE

TEXTUAL ANALYSIS

CHAPTER 1

Jane Eyre tells her own story as she remembers it. At the beginning of the book she was a ten-year-old orphan living with her relatives, the Reeds, as a dependent. The Reeds, landowning gentry in the north of England, were comfortably off. Mrs. Reed, a widow, spoiled her three children, Eliza, Georgiana, and John. John, now fourteen, had become particularly obnoxious, a fat, greedy, unwholesome bully. However, in his mother's eyes he could do no wrong and was allowed to stay home from school because his mother thought he was delicate. When the story opens, on a sombre, rainy November day, Jane was feeling deeply her position as an outsider. Mrs. Reed was on the sofa by the fire "with her darlings about her," while the shy and lonely Jane was made to sit apart from the others until she was ready to be more "sociable and ... sprightly." Jane took refuge in a small breakfast room where there were books. Sitting crosslegged on the window sill behind the heavy scarlet curtains, she felt she was "in double retirement." For a while she looked out at the "wet lawn and storm-beat shrubs" and listened to the "lamentable blast" of the wind.

COMMENT

Notice how quickly Charlotte Brontë has emphasized her heroine's aloneness. First we see Jane looking from the far side of the room at a family in which she has no part, then observing them from her hiding place. Charlotte is fond of these "outsider looking-in" effects. You will find another in Chapter 28. Notice also how few words Charlotte needs to establish a dreary, stormy winter day and the winter landscape. When you read *Wuthering Heights*, you will find that her sister Emily is also adept at "scattering" descriptive touches in her narrative-touches brief and casual, but clear and vivid. Contrast the long "set piece" descriptions in Scott. Notice also the coldness and bareness suggested by the opening lines of the novel - in harmony with Jane's mood.

Like many children who read to escape from a miserable everyday life, Jane was very imaginative. As she looked at the pictures in Bewick's *History of British Birds*, she saw in her mind's eye far-off scenes (some of which remind us of Coleridge's "Ancient Mariner") - the "deathwhite realms" of Arctic ice, a shipwreck under a ghostly moon, phantom vessels becalmed, and a "black horned thing" on a rock. "With Bewick on my knee," she writes, "I was then happy: happy at least in my way. I feared nothing but interruption, and that came too soon."

John Reed, calling Jane "bad animal," frightened her from her retreat; he insisted she address him as "Master Reed," and hit her for what he called her impudence and sneaking ways. "You have no business to take our books," he cried, "you are a dependent, mama says; you have no money; your father left you none; you ought to beg, and not to live here with gentlemen's children like us, and eat the same meals we do, and wear clothes at our mama's expense. Now, I'll teach you to rummage my bookshelves: for they are mine; all the house belongs to me, or will be in a few years." He hurled the heavy book at her, knocking her down so that she cut her head. Now pain and anger gave Jane courage to speak out. She called her tormentor a tyrant and slavedriver like one of the evil Roman emperors. When John attacked her, she flew at him like a fury. The servants had to separate them and Mrs. Reed directed, "Take her away to the red-room and lock her in there."

COMMENT

Later you will see that *Jane Eyre* is something of a Cinderella story. What Cinderella motif do you find in this first chapter? Note that seeing Jane as a child and watching her grow up involves us in her story more deeply than if we first saw her as an adult.

JANE EYRE

TEXTUAL ANALYSIS

CHAPTER 2

"I resisted all the way; a new thing for me," writes Jane, "... like any other rebel slave, I felt resolved, in my desperation, to go all lengths." The servant Bessie and Abbot, the ladies' maid (called an "Abigail" - see I Samuel 25:24), said she was like a mad cat and reproached her for striking her benefactress' son. Bessie reminded her, not unkindly, that the Reeds were rich and she was poor and that if Mrs. Reed turned her out she would have to go to the poorhouse. She ought to be humble and agreeable. Abbot threatened her: "God will punish her: he might strike her dead in the midst of her tantrums, and then where would she go?"

COMMENT

Observe the character contrast between the two servants. It was not uncommon in those days to threaten naughty children with hell-fire. (See Life and Chapter 4.)

The servants left Jane locked up alone in the bedroom, so-called because the bed and the windows were heavily draped with dark red curtains, the furniture was mahogany and other furnishings were in tones of sombre red. The room was chilly, silent and remote. To Jane it seemed a solemn and frightening place, because Mr. Reed died there nine years ago. There his body had lain until the funeral and "since that day, a sense of dreary consecration had guarded it from frequent intrusion." Jane tried the door, but it was locked. She saw her own white face and frightened eyes in the mirror, looking like a ghost or mischievous spirit. She thought of Bessie's tales of phantoms haunting belated travelers.

COMMENT

In the description of the red-room and of Jane's fears, notice Charlotte Brontë's faculty for creating an atmosphere of fear and tension. Jane's imagination, fed by Bessie's tales of the supernatural, only increased her suffering. (The idea of a person under tension being terrified by her own face in the mirror is also used by Emily Brontë in *Wuthering Heights*, Chapter 12, where the older Catherine frightens herself into near-insanity.) "I was a discord at Gateshead Hall; I was like nobody there; I had nothing in harmony with Mrs. Reed or her children." She saw that she had not the temperament to appeal to Mrs. Reed. "I know that had I been a sanguine, brilliant, careless, exacting, handsome, romping child, ... Mrs. Reed would have endured my presence more complacently..."

The rain still beat on the window, the wind howled. "Daylight began to forsake the red-room. It was past four o'clock, and the beclouded afternoon was tending to drear twilight ... I grew by degrees cold as stone and then my courage sank." She remembered that everybody said she was wicked. What if she should die? She dwelt with dread on the corpse of her uncle, buried in the vault of Gateshead Church. On his deathbed he had made Mrs. Reed promise to look after Jane, his sister's child. He would have been kind. "I began to recall what I had heard of dead men, troubled in their graves by the violation of their last wishes." She wondered fearfully if the ghost of Mr. Reed, troubled by the wrongs being done to his niece, would rise before her. A chance gleam of light deepened the expectation. "... Shaken as my nerves were by agitation, I thought the swift-darting beam was a herald of some coming vision from another world. My heart beat thick, my head grew hot; a sound filled my ears, which I deemed the rushing of wings." She shook the lock and screamed in terror and seized Bessie's hand when she and Abbot came in. But Abbot did not understand or care about her terror. "She had screamed out on purpose ... to bring us all here. I know her naughty tricks," she said, and Mrs. Reed supported her; "It is my duty to show you that tricks will not answer: you will now stay here an hour longer, and it is only on condition of perfect submission and stillness that I shall liberate you then." "Oh aunt, have pity! Forgive me! I cannot endure it! Let me be punished some other way!" Jane cried, but Mrs. Reed merely found the emotional violence repulsive. Impatient of Jane's wildness and tears, she pushed her in, locked the door and went away. Jane lost consciousness.

COMMENT

Observe that Jane, in spite of her intense feelings, can be objective enough to see why Mrs. Reed does not like her. For another vivid picture of a child without status and without a protector, read the early chapters of Charles Dickens' *David Copperfield*. We have in this book and in *Jane Eyre* two of the earliest rounded, detailed pictures of childhood.

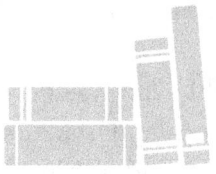

JANE EYRE

TEXTUAL ANALYSIS

CHAPTER 3

Waking from a nightmare and still in a state of terror, Jane thought she saw "a terrible red glare, crossed with thick, black bars," like a prison window. (Compare Coleridge's description of the sun peering through dungeon bars in Part IV of "The Ancient Mariner.") However, she realized someone was lifting and holding her gently. In a few minutes her mind cleared. She realized that the glare was the nursery fire and that Bessie and Mr. Lloyd the apothecary (i.e., chemist) were with her. She felt comforted because someone from outside was there. Her heart sank when Mr. Lloyd went, but Bessie was kindly and wondered if Jane had, in fact, seen a ghost. There were rumors of mysterious rapings, a mysterious light over Mr. Reed's grave, so Bessie was glad to have another servant sleep with her. Jane could not sleep: "ear, eye, and mind were alike strained by dread: such dread as children only can feel." She woke in a low-spirited frame of mind, "a wretchedness," she said, "which kept drawing from me silent tears; no sooner had I wiped one salt deep from my cheek than another followed." She begged for *Gulliver's Travels*, but it did not comfort her as usual - "all was eerie and dreary; the giants were gaunt goblins, the pigmies malevolent and fearful imps, Gulliver a most desolate wanderer in most dread and dangerous regions." Bessie's doleful **ballad**, with its **refrain** "poor orphan child" only made her cry.

COMMENT

Notice how the hints of supernatural events in the neighborhood and Bessie's song add to the atmosphere.

Next day Mr. Lloyd called again and tried to get the rather inarticulate Jane to tell him why she was so unhappy and whether she had some other relatives she could live with. Aunt Reed had only mentioned "some poor low relatives called Eyre" (we shall hear more of them later), but Jane does not feel heroic enough to live with poor people. Later it is explained that when Mr. Eyre, Jane's father, and the rich Miss Reed (the dead Uncle Reed's sister) fell in love, the Reed family opposed the match because Eyre was only a poor clergyman. The couple did marry, but the Reeds refused to allow any of their family's money to go to Mrs. Eyre. Two years later both the Eyres died of typhus, leaving the orphan Jane a dependent of the Reeds. Mr. Lloyd was of the opinion that Jane badly needed a change of scene, and she agreed that she would like to go away to school.

COMMENT

Notice that we learn about Jane from the comments which other people make about her. Notice that Mr. Lloyd's attitude is a moderate one-midway between the family's hard-heartedness and Jane's own deep feeling. It helps to give the reader a balanced point of view.

JANE EYRE

TEXTUAL ANALYSIS

CHAPTER 4

Nearly three months went by Jane's health improved, but she was kept more and more apart from the Reed children. However, the spirit of revolt, which had earlier made her defy John, was still alive. When he tried again to torment her, she hit him on the nose as hard as she could; and when the blubbering bully ran to his mother, Jane defied her, too. "What would Uncle Reed say to you if he were alive?" she cried. "My Uncle Reed is in heaven and can see all you do and think; and so can papa and mama: they know how you shut me up all day long, and how you wish me dead." Jane was punished for her defiance and excluded from the Christmas parties. She was left to comfort herself with her doll ("human beings must love something") and with a little affection from the maid, Bessie, who occasionally told her stories and brought her treats from the kitchen.

COMMENT

Notice that although much of the time the story is so vivid that we feel that the events are taking place before us, at times the narrator seems to be looking back at her childhood. We call this point of view "retrospective." For example, Jane as the supposed narrator thinks back on her feelings as a child about the doll, Bessie, and her defiance of Aunt Reed. Look for other examples. (Before you read on, re-read the Introduction.)

One morning in mid-January, Jane was called to the breakfast room. There she found a clergyman, the Reverend Brocklehurst, with her aunt. The tall, black-coated gentleman, with his stern, mask-life face and huge teeth, seemed like a cold black marble pillar. Mrs. Reed had clearly already told him that Jane was a bad child, for he asked her, "Do you know where the wicked go after death?"

"They go to hell," was my ready and orthodox answer.

"And what is hell? Can you tell me that?"

"A pit full of fire."

"And should you like to fall into that pit, and to be burning there forever?"

"No sir."

"What must you do to avoid it?"

I deliberated a moment; my answer, when it did come, was objectionable: "I must keep in good health, and not die."

Mr. Brocklehurst reminded her that many children die young. He reproved her because she did not like all the books of the Bible and told her of a little boy who preferred learning psalms to eating ginger cookies. "Psalms are not interesting," declared Jane unwisely, and Mr. Brocklehurst replies,

"That proves you have a wicked heart; and you must pray to God to change it: to give you a heart of flesh."

Mrs. Reed now impressed on Mr. Brocklehurst that Jane was a naughty, lying child and that she should be brought up to be useful and humble. He assured her that the school was a strict and austere one, and departed, leaving with Jane a pamphlet on the "sudden death of Martha G., a naughty child addicted to falsehood and deceit." (See under Brocklehurst.)

Jane, who had been much distressed by being called a liar, could not help speaking out to Mrs. Reed: "I am not deceitful: if I were, I should say I love you, but I declare I do not love you: I dislike you the worst of anybody in the world except John Reed; and this book about the liar, you may give to your girl, Georgiana, for it is she who tells lies, and not I ... I am glad you are no relation of mine: I will never call you aunt again as long as I live. I will never come to see you when I am grown up; and if anyone asks me how I liked you, and how you treated me, I will say the very thought of you makes me sick, and that you treated me with miserable cruelty ... You think I have no feelings, and that I can do without one bit of love or kindness; but I cannot live so: and you have no pity." Mrs. Reed was startled at Jane's passionate outburst and left her alone. Jane had won the battle, but suffered the inevitable reaction: guilt and remorse. (Notice again the retrospective comment.) Fortunately Bessie was in a kindly mood, and her delightful songs and stories gave Jane a gleam of sunshine.

COMMENT

Notice the realistic way in which the child Jane suffers from a sense of deflation after her "victory" over her aunt. Notice too how Charlotte Brontë uses Bessie's comments to point out to us that changes are going on in Jane. Read the early chapters of *David Copperfield* and compare the Murdstones' use of religion as a weapon with Mr. Brocklehurst's. (For the text about "a heart of flesh," see Ezekiel 11:19.)

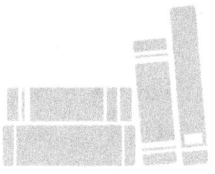

JANE EYRE

TEXTUAL ANALYSIS

CHAPTER 5

....

Up and dressed while it was still dark, by six o'clock Jane was ready for the coach. Her teeth chattered in the cold as her trunk was hoisted up, the coachman urged on his horses, Bessie and Gateshead disappeared, and Jane was embarked on the fifty-mile journey to Lowood School.

On arrival, Jane was greeted by Miss Temple, the kindly superintendent of Lowood, and by a careworn, overworked assistant. In the large classroom she saw about eighty girls, aged from nine or ten to twenty, studying their lessons by candlelight. After a meager supper (oatcake and water) and prayers, the girls retired to long rows of beds in the dormitory (here - "sleeping rooms," not a separate building). In the morning, Jane soon learned that the day's progress was marked by bells. A bell roused the girls before dawn to line up for the cold wash in the tin basins; a bell called them to the classroom; another bell rang for prayers; and, after the repetition of the Collect (the special prayer for the day in the Church of England) and some Bible verses and an hour-long reading from the Scriptures, fourth bell called them to breakfast. On this particular day the porridge was so burned that no one could eat it.

Punctually at nine, all the girls were ranged on benches down the sides of the schoolroom. All, even the oldest, wore brown high-necked frocks, woolen stockings, and heavy shoes. Miss Temple appeared and lessons began. At twelve, Miss Temple, on her own responsibility, had bread and cheese brought out for the hungry girls, who were then sent into the wet garden to play. Jane got acquainted with Helen Burns, a gentle, bookloving girl of thirteen who explained to her that Lowood was a school for orphans, in effect a charity school, since the rather small sum paid by relatives had to be supplemented by contributions from benevolent well-wishers. The institution was run by Mr. Brocklehurst, whose mother rebuilt a portion of the house. Before Jane went to a dinner of "indifferent potatoes" and "rusty meat," she read the inscription over the door: "Let your light so shine before men that they may see your good works, and glorify your Father which is in heaven." - St. Matt. 5:16.

COMMENT

Note the **irony** implied in the contrast between the spirit of Jesus' saying and the actual conditions at Lowood. Note, too, the vividness with which the sights, sounds, and smells of the school are depicted.

JANE EYRE

TEXTUAL ANALYSIS

CHAPTER 6

....

Next morning the girls could not wash because the water in the jugs was frozen. By the time the long prayers and Bible readings were over, Jane was chilled to the bone. The day seemed very long, and the many different lessons confused her. She was also upset because a particularly strict teacher, Miss Scatcherd, kept up a constant stream of criticism of Helen Burns. Eventually she whipped her because her fingernails were dirty. Helen accepted her punishment meekly. Jane was very indignant on Helen's behalf and declared if she were whipped she would grab the rod and break it. Helen defended Miss Scatcherd, saying that she was only trying to correct her faults, and reminded Jane that the Bible tells us to return good for evil. Jane said she couldn't bear such a humiliation, but Helen reproved her: "it is weak and silly to say you cannot bear what it is your fate to be required to bear." She said she had many faults: "I am ... slatternly ... I am careless; I forget rules; I read when I should learn my lessons and sometimes I say, like you, I cannot bear to be subject to systematic arrangements." Even to please Miss Temple, she could not always be good and attentive, but let her thoughts wander. Jane could not understand such meekness; experience had taught her to fight: "When we are struck at without reason, we should strike back again very hard; I am sure we should - so hard as to teach the person who struck us never to do so again ... I must dislike those who, whatever I do to please them, persist in disliking me; I must resist those who punish me unjustly. It is as natural as that I should love those who show me affection, or submit to punishment when I feel it is deserved." "Heathens and savage tribes hold that doctrine," replied Helen, "but Christians and civilized nations disown it. "She bade Jane follow Christ's example, "Love your enemies; bless them that curse you; do good to them that hate you and despitefully use you." Jane could not accept this difficult ideal. She told Helen how harshly she had been treated by Mrs. Reed. Helen thought Jane made too much of her wrongs. "What a singularly deep impression her injustice seems to have made on your heart! No ill-usage so brands its record on my feelings. Would you not be happier if you tried to forget her severity, together with the passionate emotions it excited? Life appears to me too short to be spent in nursing animosity, or registering wrongs." She reminded Jane that human life is short, that before long they would be "putting off their corruptible bodies ... only the spark of the spirit will remain." Eternity, insisted Helen, was "a rest - a mighty home, not a terror and an abyss." She said she did not fear death and declared, "I live in calm, looking to the end."

COMMENT

Notice the sharp contrast between the attitudes of the two girls. Remember that Helen is based on Charlotte's dead sister Maria (see Life.)

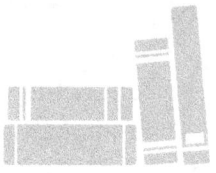

JANE EYRE

TEXTUAL ANALYSIS

CHAPTER 7

Jane found her first quarter at Lowood long and trying. In spite of cold weather and heavy snow, the girls were made to stay outdoors for an hour each day, although they had neither boots nor gloves. Food was scanty, and the bigger girls used often to "coax or menace" the younger ones out of their portions. Sundays were marked chiefly by a cold walk to church for two services in an icy building and by learning the Catechism and the Beatitudes (Matthew 5:2–11) by heart.

Meanwhile Jane dreaded the return of Mr. Brocklehurst, for she remembered his promise to Mrs. Reed to warn the school that her niece was a liar. When he did come, he inspected the washing on the line to see if the stockings were mended and found out from the laundress that more changes of clothing had been given out than his rules allowed. He rebuked Miss Temple for the extra lunch of bread and cheese and insisted that one girl's red curls must be shorn off. These remarks were accompanied by many **allusions** to the Bible. While he had been talking, his wife and daughters were conducting "a rummaging scrutiny of the rooms upstairs." They appeared in fashionable dresses and hats trimmed with ostrich feathers just as Mr. Brocklehurst concluded his observations on the sinfulness of vanity.

COMMENT

Note the **allusion** to Jesus' dry comment on the Pharisees who ceremonially cleanse the outside of the cup but inwardly are full of sin. Incidentally, the fashionable attire of the Brocklehurst girls is certainly an addition to history. Mr. Carus Wilson's children were much too young for such finery when Charlotte was at Cowan Bridge.

All this happened while Jane had been trying to hide behind her slate, but in her nervousness she dropped it with a bang. This reminded Mr. Brocklehurst of her presence and of his promise to Mrs. Reed. Making Jane stand up on a stool, he told the entire school that "this girl, who might be one of God's own lambs, is a little castaway; not a member of the true flock ..." The other students must beware of her example, and the teachers must "punish her body to save her soul," for she was a liar and an ingrate. As a punishment, she must stand on the stool for half an hour, and no one must speak to her all day. By this time, Jane was full of shame and fury, but Helen Burns made an excuse to pass her and give her a smile of encouragement. "What a smile!" recalls Jane, for it gave her new courage. "I mastered the rising hysteria, lifted my head, and took a firm stand on the stool."

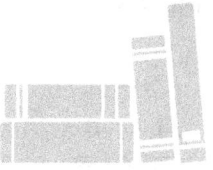

JANE EYRE

TEXTUAL ANALYSIS

CHAPTER 8

....

However, the heroic mood did not last, and five o'clock found Jane weeping passionately. She was afraid the girls and teachers would despise her. Helen tried to comfort her by assuring her that they would be much more likely to sympathize with her and that Mr. Brocklehurst was not much liked. Still afraid that her reputation with the other girls was hurt, Jane cried, "If others don't love me, I would rather die than live." "You think too much of the love of human beings," Helen warned her; ... "there is an invisible world ... angels see our tortures, recognize our innocence..."

Just then Miss Temple invited the two girls to her comfortable room, sympathized with what Jane told of her situation at the Reeds, and promised that if Mr. Lloyd confirmed her story, she would be publicly cleared. Meanwhile she was much concerned with Helen's cough and painful chest, though Helen made light of them. Next, Jane listened enthralled to the brilliant conversation between the two. "They conversed of things I had never heard of: of nations and times past; of countries far away; of secrets of nature discovered or guessed at. They spoke of books: how many they had read!" Jane's astonishment at Helen's eloquence and knowledge reached its height when she found her friend could read Latin.

COMMENT

In picturing Helen's deeply religious nature and her intellectual gifts, Charlotte continues to draw on her memories of her sister Maria. There is other evidence (chiefly from Mr. Brontë) that Maria was an exceptional child. Mr. Brontë discussed politics and current events with her on an adult level.

A week later Miss Temple heard from Mr. Lloyd, assembled the school, and announced that the charge that Jane was untruthful had been proved false. Jane, "relieved of a grievous load," worked hard at her studies, did well, and was allowed to start French and drawing. She took great pleasure in her achievements. "I would not now have exchanged Lowood with all its privations, for Gateshead and its daily luxuries."

JANE EYRE

TEXTUAL ANALYSIS

CHAPTER 9

....

In any case, as spring came on, the hardships at Lowood lessened. Snowdrops and crocuses peeped out, oak and elm put forth fresh leaves, the brook sparkled in the sun, and Jane began to enjoy the beautiful Lakeland scenery. But a typhus epidemic broke out at the school. Malnutrition and cold had lowered the girls' resistance and forty-five out of eighty caught the infection. Some went home to die, some died at school and were buried there. Helen Burns, Jane heard, was ill too, not of typhus, but of tuberculosis. Jane did not realize how serious this could be until she heard that Helen was really dying. "I experienced a shock of horrors, then a strong thrill of grief, then a desire - a necessity to see her; ... I must give her one last kiss, exchange with her one last word." That night she tiptoed up to where Helen was lying. Helen was calm, cheerful, ready to die, and pleased that Jane had come to see her. Jane was in tears, but Helen begged her not to grieve. "I am going to God ... God is my friend: I love him; I believe he loves me ... You will come to the same region of happiness." Comforted, Jane went to sleep on Helen's shoulder and woke without realizing that her friend had passed quietly away in the night. Looking back, Jane thinks of her grave and the marble tablet inscribed with the promise "Resurgam" (I shall arise).

COMMENT

Mr. Brontë records that Maria "exhibited during her illness many symptoms of a heart under Divine influence." Again the character of Helen is drawn from life. You will realize, though, that not every detail in the novel is exact; for example, the epidemic was probably not typhus, since only one child at Cowan Bridge actually died, and Maria is buried, not near the school, as in *Jane Eyre*, but in Haworth churchyard. Beyond question, however, Charlotte relived her grief and anger at the death of her sister when she wrote this chapter.

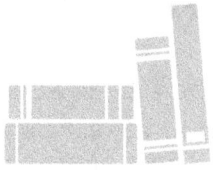

JANE EYRE

TEXTUAL ANALYSIS

CHAPTER 10

The epidemic drew attention to the bad conditions at Lowood. Public opinion was aroused and Mr. Brocklehurst was obliged to give up some of his authority. Things improved; the school became "a truly useful and noble institution," and Jane spent eight happy years there, the last two as a teacher. But after Miss Temple left to be married, Jane felt unsettled and restless. Looking from her window at the blue hills and the winding road, she realized that there was a great world beyond and longed to explore it, "to seek real knowledge of life beyond its perils." She longed for liberty, or if that was impossible, a "new servitude." She quickly laid her plans. Without telling her companions, she advertised for a post and was offered one at thirty pounds a year (double her salary at Lowood) to teach one little girl. Just as she was ready to leave, her old acquaintance, Bessie, now married, came to see her. She was much impressed with Jane's piano-playing, painting, and knowledge of French and declared that the Miss Reeds were not nearly as accomplished. The Miss Reeds, incidentally, quarreled constantly since Eliza gave away

Georgiana's plans to elope. John Reed failed his course at college and was a dissipated youth, a great anxiety to his mother. Bessie also inquired whether Jane had ever heard from her relatives the Eyres. Seven years before, she explained, a Mr. Eyre, Jane's father's brother, inquired at Gateshead for Jane and was disappointed not to find her there. He was sailing for Madeira shortly and could not come to Lowood. He struck Bessie as "quite a gentleman." Jane had never heard from him.

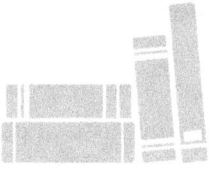

JANE EYRE

TEXTUAL ANALYSIS

CHAPTER 11

Jane's new home, Thornfield Hall, was the manor house of a village near the industrial town of Millcote (Leeds). By a cosy fire, Mrs. Fairfax, "the neatest imaginable little elderly lady," gave her employee a warm welcome. From her Jane learned that her pupil was a little French girl, Adele, ward to Mr. Rochester, the absentee owner of Thornfield. Adele was delighted to find that her new governess could speak her language and proceeded to sing and recite in a professional manner taught her by her mother.

Thornfield Hall, a beautifully furnished house, was three stories high, with picturesque battlements from which one could see the surrounding countryside spread out like a map. Rooks cawed and wheeled about the house and alighted in the meadows, where stood the great knotted thorn trees which gave the place its name. Exploring the third floor, Jane found it furnished with carved chests, ancient beds, and rich hangings. The atmosphere was hushed, gloomy and mysterious. Suddenly from behind one of the closed black doors she heard a mysterious, unnatural laugh. "It was a curious laugh; distinct, formal, mirthless." The sound chilled Jane, but Mrs. Fairfax explained that it was just Grace Poole, who sewed in one of the rooms. Grace appeared, "a set, square-made figure ... with a hard, plain face," and for the moment Jane was satisfied.

COMMENT

The Angrian stories contain several **episodes** in which a girl comes to a strange house while the master is away; but the **episode** here is more realistically treated. Thornfield is based on Charlotte's recollections of Ellen's home, Rydings, and of Norton Conyers near Ripon.

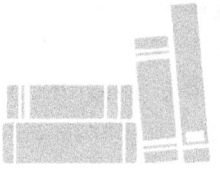

JANE EYRE

TEXTUAL ANALYSIS

CHAPTER 12

Three months went by. Under Jane's teaching Adele became less spoiled and more obedient and teachable. Mrs. Fairfax continued to be pleasant and placid. But Jane, though aware that her lot was a comfortable one, was restless and longed for a more vivid experience of life. The only thing that relieved this sense of frustration for Jane was to walk up and down the passage on the third floor while her mind dwelt on "whatever bright visions" rose before it. From these visions she invented a never-ending tale "which," she recalls, "my imagination created and narrated continuously: quickened with all of incident, life, fire, feeling that I desired and had not in my actual existence."

COMMENT

Here Charlotte is again using her own experience, her delight in the Angrian writings, to describe a facet of her heroine's character.

In a passionate aside, Jane declares (and Charlotte was surely speaking through her heroine here) that women should not be criticized for wanting more out of life than "making puddings and knitting stockings ... playing on the piano and embroidering bags." "Women are supposed to be very calm generally: but women feel just as men feel; they need exercise for their faculties, and a field for their efforts as much as their brothers do; they suffer from too rigid a constraint, too absolute a stagnation, precisely as men would suffer." From time to time when Jane was alone with her thoughts, she heard again the mysterious laugh. Yet when she saw Grace Poole with a tray, basin, or pot of porter in her hand, her prosaic appearance certainly seemed at variance with the strange laugh.

One frosty afternoon Jane set out to take a letter to the village post office. After sitting on a stile to watch the sun go down, she was about to go on her way by the light of the rising moon when she heard a clatter of hoofs in the lane. For a moment she feared it might be a Gytrash - a spirit which could take the form of various animals - but this horse had a rider and therefore could not be a spirit. Just as she came to this conclusion, the horse slipped on the ice and he and his rider crashed to the ground. The dog with them barked and appeared to summon Jane to help his master. Horse and rider both struggled to their feet, but the man had sprained his ankle. Jane offered to run for help, but the gentleman would not hear of this. He did, however, lean on Jane's shoulder while he secured his horse's bridle, then mounted and galloped away.

Jane reflected on this passing encounter with the stern, dark stranger. "My help had been needed and claimed; I had given it; I was pleased to have done something." To help satisfied something in her nature. With rising emotion she watched the moon going up the night sky "in solemn march," attended by "trembling stars." Her heart, too, trembled with longing for a richer and fuller life. She felt reluctant to return to the dull life at Thornfield. However, when she did return, she discovered that the mysterious stranger was none other than owner of the hall, Mr. Edward Fairfax Rochester.

COMMENT

It is important to notice two things in this chapter: 1) the insistence on the rights of women to a complete and full life, which has already been mentioned and 2) the care with which Charlotte sets the scene for encounters between Jane and Rochester - here the moonlit frosty night with the majestic winter sky. You will notice other instances later in the novel.

JANE EYRE

TEXTUAL ANALYSIS

CHAPTER 13

Next day it was clear that Thornfield would be much livelier after the master's arrival. All day tenants and agents came and went. Jane and Adele were summoned to take tea with Mr. Rochester at six o'clock. While Adele clamored for her "cadeaux" (presents), Jane observed by the light of the candles her traveler of the night before. He was squarely built, his face "made squarer by the horizontal sweep of his black hair," his mouth grim and his figure broad-chested and sturdy. Jane was intrigued by his behavior. He did not trouble to look up when she came in and did not reply to Mrs. Fairfax's remarks on his busy day, though eventually he did tell Jane that he could see that Adele had improved under her teaching. Jane found that his rudeness put her at her ease just as his tendency to give orders had done the night before. He questioned her minutely and rather arrogantly about her connections and her education. She answered meekly enough, but was frank in her criticisms of Mr. Brocklehurst. He put her ability on the piano to the test ("You play a little, I see") and had her bring out her folder of drawings, which he scrutinized in detail, asking if she had been happy doing them and contended with the results. Jane explained that she had been absorbed in making the pictures, but not satisfied: "I was tormented by the contrast between my ideas and my handiwork; in each case I had imagined something which I was quite powerless to realize." Suddenly tiring of the conversation, Mr. Rochester dismissed them both: "What are you about, Miss Eyre, to let Adele sit up so long? Take her to bed."

Jane asked Mrs. Fairfax why Mr. Rochester was so "changeful and abrupt." Mrs. Fairfax explained that allowance should be made for his manner, because "painful thoughts" and "family troubles" harassed him. She hinted that Mr. Rochester's father and elder brother, Rowland, now dead, had taken steps to place him in "a painful position, for the sake of making his fortune," but what these steps were and what this position was she could not say. "No wonder he shuns the old place [Thornfield]," she concluded, and Jane was obliged to drop the subject.

COMMENT

Humor is not very frequent in Charlotte Brontë's books, but there is some in this chapter as Jane and Mr. Rochester talk solemnly of elves and bewitchings and of Mr. Brocklehurst, quite over Mrs. Fairfax's head.

Notice that Charlotte, like Emily in *Wuthering Heights*, likes to create an atmosphere of mystery about the past, mystery which is gradually explained and which affects what happens in the present.

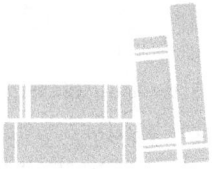

JANE EYRE

TEXTUAL ANALYSIS

CHAPTER 14

Some days later Jane and Adele were again invited to join Mr. Rochester, this time after dinner. They sat cozily by the fire as the rain beat against the windows, and Mr. Rochester, in a rather genial mood, again turned his attention to Jane. "Do you think me handsome?" he asked. "No, sir," replied Jane without thinking; then wished she had said something less blunt. But Mr. Rochester was not annoyed. He begged her to "read" the contours of his head. (Charlotte Brontë was interested in phrenology, which some people considered quite scientific at that time.) Jane found intelligence and conscience, but not benevolence; he admitted that benevolence was not his strong point, but hinted that misfortune had embittered him. When he wondered if his informality and lack of conventional good manners would annoy Jane, she replied that she would "never mistake informality for insolence; the one I rather like, the other nothing free-born would submit to." Much struck by the independence of her reply, Mr. Rochester hinted further that his past had been wicked and that he envied her "clean conscience" and "unpolluted memory." "Remorse," he declared, "is the poison of life." "Repentance is said to be its cure, sir," replied Jane - " ... If you tried hard, you would in time find it possible to become what you yourself would approve." Finally, getting rather out of her depth, Jane decided to put Adele to bed. The child had meanwhile opened her presents and was dressed in one of them - a rose-colored satin dress in which she danced across the room. "Coquetry runs in her blood," commented her guardian. She was very like her French mother, who in the past had charmed much gold from his pockets. He was only rearing the "French floweret," he said, on the principle of "expiating numerous sins, great or small, by one good work."

COMMENT

Lord Byron, the Romantic poet, set the fashion for Byronic heroes such as Mr. Rochester and Heathcliff in Emily Brontë's *Wuthering Heights*. A Byronic hero is a man with splendid personal qualities who yet feels he is doomed by an unkind fate, cursed by being in a kind of Limbo between God and man. Like Milton's Satan in *Paradise Lost* he is a sort of "archangel ruined." He usually is a man of great courage, and, though convinced he is cursed, fights to the end.

JANE EYRE

TEXTUAL ANALYSIS

CHAPTER 15

Remarking that Jane was born to be a recipient of confidences, Mr. Rochester one day recounted to her the story of his infatuation for Adele's mother. Celine, Varens, a French opera-dancer. "I installed her in a hotel; gave her a complete establishment of servants, a carriage, cashmeres, dentelles [laces], etc. In short I began the process of ruining myself in the received style ..." However, one evening he discovered her with a rival, a young officer. He broke off with Celine, wounded the officer in the arm (duels were then still held in some quarters to be a matter of honor), and, much later, undertook to look after Adele, whom her mother had abandoned. Though he did not think she was his child, he "took the poor thing out of the slime and mud of Paris, and transplanted it here to grow up clean in the wholesome soil of an English country garden." Midway in this discourse, which was taking place in the beech avenue outside the hall, Mr. Rochester glared up at the battlements, ground his teeth, and said that destiny seemed to have been standing by a beech tree like one of the witches from Macbeth saying to him, "You like Thornfield? ... Like it if you can! Like it if you dare!"

In spite of his mysterious way of talking at times and in spite of his often proud and sarcastic arrogance, Jane grew fond of the master of the hall and saw much good in him. She knew that something troubled him deeply, something connected with Thornfield. "I grieved of his grief, whatever that was, and would have given much to assuage it." She dreaded lest he leave. Thornfield, for she would find life joyless without his friendship.

One night a strange, frightening thing happened. Just as the clock struck two, Jane heard the "demonic laugh." Something gurgled and moaned on the stairs. Frightened, Jane slipped into a dress and out into the hall. There was a strong smell of burning, and smoke poured from Mr. Rochester's room. Jane rushed in and, unable to rouse him, smothered the flames with the water from the jug and basin. His comment as he woke in a pool of water was typical: "In the name of all the elves of Christendom, is that Jane Eyre? What have you done with me, witch, sorceress?" But he grew grave when he heard her story, disappeared to the third floor, and returned even graver. He seemed to agree with Jane that it was Grace Poole who laughed so peculiarly, and he let her think Grace was responsible for the fire. However, the origin of the fire really remained a mystery, and the victim begged Jane not to speak of it to anyone.

He did not let Jane go without taking her hand and thanking her. "You have saved my life: I have a pleasure in owing you so immense a debt. I cannot say more ... I knew you would do me good ... I saw it in your eyes when I first beheld you: their expression and smile did not ... strike delight to my very inmost heart so for nothing." All this was said while he was still holding Jane's hand, but finally she escaped to her own room. "Till morning dawned I was tossed on a buoyant but unquiet sea, where billows of trouble rolled under surges of joy ... Too feverish to rest, I rose as soon as day dawned."

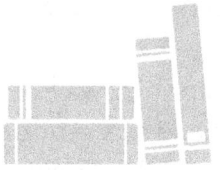

JANE EYRE

TEXTUAL ANALYSIS

CHAPTER 16

Next morning Jane both hoped and dreaded to see Mr. Rochester, but he did not appear. What did surprise her was to see Grace Poole, "staid and taciturn-looking as usual," sitting in Mr. Rochester's room sewing on curtain-rings. Questioned, she said that Mr. Rochester had fallen asleep with his candle lit and thus set the curtains on fire, but fortunately was able to put it out with the water from the washstand. Jane, who still thought that Grace was the culprit, was thunderstruck, and declared that she heard the strange laugh in the night. But Grace insisted that she must have been dreaming. Completely baffled by Grace's imperturbable manner, Jane wondered what the secret of her power on Mr. Rochester could be? Why had she not been given in to custody or at least dismissed? Could she have been a past mistress of Mr. Rochester? She was so unattractive that this seemed hardly likely. Jane longed to see her master and question him about the mystery. However, at teatime she learned from Mrs. Fairfax that he had gone for a week or so to an elegant house party on the far side of Millcote. Mrs. Fairfax enlarged on Mr. Rochester's social gifts and popularity in society. She also described the beautiful Blanche Ingram, who sang and played the piano and indeed in the past had sung duets with Mr. Rochester.

Alone, Jane went over what she had been told and scolded herself for letting her feelings run away with her since the night before. "You," she said to herself, "a favorite with Mr. Rochester? You gifted with the power of pleasing him? You of importance to him in any way? Go! Your folly sickens me." And although Mrs. Fairfax had denied that Mr. Rochester was planning to marry Lady Blanche, the difference in their ages being too great, Jane devised a punishment for herself. She drew a faithful portrait of herself, labeled it "Portrait of a Governess, disconnected, poor, and plain," and painted a delicate miniature of Lady Blanche as she imagined her, calling the portrait "an accomplished lady of rank." The contrast was designed to keep her feelings in check, for, as she reminded herself: "It does good to no woman to be flattered by her superior, who cannot possibly intend to marry her; and it is madness in all women to let a secret love kindle within them …"

COMMENT

Some biographers think that this observation and indeed the general picture of frustrated love is based on Charlotte's own experience. (See Life.)

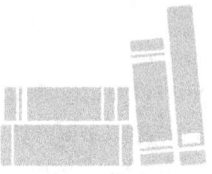

JANE EYRE

TEXTUAL ANALYSIS

CHAPTER 17

....

As the days passed and Mr. Rochester remained absent, Jane felt "a strange chill and failing at the heart," although she reminded herself, "He is not of your order: keep to your caste and be too self-respecting to lavish the love of a whole heart ... where such a gift is not wanted." After about two weeks, however, Mr. Rochester wrote that he would return shortly bringing house guests. Extra servants were hired to clean the house and furnishings until they sparkled, and Adele was freed from lessons as Jane had to help Mrs. Fairfax and the cook to prepare pastries, game, and desserts. From a conversation she overheard, she gathered yet another hint that there was a mystery connected with Grace Poole - a mystery from which she was excluded, since the servants fell silent when they saw her listening.

At last the cavalcade appeared, two youths on horseback, then Mr. Rochester with a lady in a purple riding habit by his side, then two carriages. Mrs. Fairfax recognized the lady in purple as the handsome and high-born Lady Blanche Ingram. Such was the excitement downstairs that at mealtime Jane was obliged to go down and forage for food, for she and Adele were quite forgotten by the servants.

On the second evening of the house party, Mr. Rochester insisted that Jane and Adele join the party in the drawing room. Among the elegant ladies, who looked "like a flock of white plumy birds," Jane was most interested in Lady Blanche, whom she found handsome, but supercilious and haughty. She also found it difficult to avoid looking at Mr. Rochester, for his strong features and his energy and vitality fascinated her in spite of herself. "I had not intended to love him: the reader knows I have wrought hard to extirpate from my soul the germs of love there detected; and now, at the first renewed view of him, they spontaneously revived, green and strong! He made me love him without looking at me." At that moment Jane realized that her master had more in common with her than with the splendid but superficial ladies, who at this moment were sneering at the whole race of governesses. Lady Blanche was flirtatiously ordering Mr. Rochester to sing a pirate song, and he was responding in kind. However, though he seemed to have forgotten Jane, he had not. Meeting her in the hallway, he commented that she looked pale and dejected and ordered her to join the house party every evening.

Comment

Jane's insistence that she and Mr. Rochester have more in common than he has with the wealthy Ingrams recalls in a somewhat modified form Emily Brontë's belief that soul-likenesses draw people together. Readers of *Wuthering Heights* will recall Cathy saying that whatever souls were made of, hers and Heathcliff's were alike.

Incidentally, notice Charlotte's predilection for a haughty mother and two haughty daughters. What other similar group have we seen?

JANE EYRE

TEXTUAL ANALYSIS

CHAPTER 18

....

"Merry days were those at Thornfield Hall," recalls Jane. When the spring weather was fine the guests amused themselves outdoors; when it was wet they played indoor games such as charades. In this game the ladies and gentlemen dressed up in clothes of past generations, stored on the third floor, and acted out words syllable by syllable. In one scene Mr. Rochester and Lady Blanche were bride and groom. Jane looked on in misery, not exactly jealous of Blanche, but deeply conscious that she was not worthy of Rochester. "She was very showy, but she was not genuine: she had a fine person, many brilliant attainments; but her mind was poor, her heart barren by nature … She was not good; she was not original: she used to repeat sounding phrases from books: she never offered, nor had, an opinion of her own." Jane was convinced, though, that Mr. Rochester would marry her "for family, perhaps for political reasons," but not for love, for "she could not charm him." If she had managed the victory at once, and he had yielded and sincerely laid his heart at her feet, I should have covered my face, turned to the wall, and (figuratively) have died to them." But as it was, Jane was forced to watch every attempt of Blanche's to charm him miss its mark. She was also troubled to find Mr. Rochester willing to marry from practical motives. Her common sense told her that class ideas and principles would justify such a marriage, but her heart dissented: "It seemed to me that, were I a gentleman like him, I would take to my bosom only such a wife as I could love ... but in other points, as well as in this, ... I was forgetting all his faults, for which I had once kept a sharp look-out ... Now I saw no bad. The sarcasm that had repelled, the harshness that had startled me once, were only like keen condiments in a choice dish." What troubled her most was that she could not be sure what the shadow was that seemed to dim his spirits.

One day when Mr. Rochester was away, some of the gentlemen were in the stables while others were with the younger ladies in the billiard room. Suddenly the sound of horses drawing a post chaise was heard. Adele thought it was her guardian returning, but it was a stranger, a fine-looking but somewhat sallow, weak-featured and apathetic gentleman, a Mr. Mason from Spanish Town, Jamaica, in the West Indies, who claimed to be an old acquaintance of Mr. Rochester. But before Mr. Rochester himself returned, a servant announced that a very persistent old gypsy woman was demanding to tell the ladies' fortunes. The older ladies hesitated, but Blanche highhandedly insisted on enjoying this diversion. However, she came back from her session with the gypsy looking very glum. The other young ladies giggled and enjoyed themselves, exclaiming, "She told us such things! She knows all about us!" While they reported on these marvels, the servant returned with the message that the gypsy wished to see the one remaining single lady. Vastly curious and excited, Jane slipped out of the room.

JANE EYRE

TEXTUAL ANALYSIS

CHAPTER 19

....

The gypsy "had on a red cloak and a black bonnet; or rather, a broad-brimmed gypsy hat, tied down with a striped handkerchief under the chin." She muttered to herself as she read a little black book by the light of the fire. In answer to her questions Jane denied being frightened or even having much faith in the gypsy's powers. The gypsy told her she was lonely, afraid to seize the happiness within her reach, unambitious in her humble desire to have a school of her own. When Jane suggested that the gypsy had gotten information from the servants, the old woman owned to knowing Grace Poole. Jane became cautious and rather evasive as the gypsy questioned her about her opinions of the house guests and of Mr. Rochester's forthcoming match. "But mother," she complained, "I did not come to hear Mr. Rochester's fortune: I came to hear my own; and you have told me nothing of it." "Your fortune is yet doubtful," replied the gypsy. She proceeded not so much to tell Jane's fortune as to read her character from her face and head. She found her eyes full of tenderness, deep feeling, and loneliness, a mouth delighting in laughter and self-expression, a forehead which indicated independence, self-respect, will-power, and the rule of reason. The forehead seemed to say "I need not sell my soul to buy bliss. I have an inward treasure ... which can keep me alive if all extraneous delights should be withheld."

COMMENT

The last sentence foreshadows Jane's integrity and conscience when she is later put to the test. Notice that though Jane is skeptical of the gypsy's palm-reading, she pays more attention when the old woman "reads her head." This again reflects Charlotte Brontë's interest in phrenology. Ironically, the very qualities the gypsy lists will prevent Rochester from forcing Jane to go away with him.

As she concluded by praising Jane's conscience, the gypsy began to speak very oddly, saying that she wished to bring Jane not misery but happiness, that she wished this moment would go on forever. Just then Jane "alert for discoveries," noticed the gypsy's hand, supple and smooth, ornamented with a broad ring. It was Mr. Rochester's hand! and sure enough, he stood before her, demanding her approval of his disguise.

"You did not act the character of a gypsy with me," said Jane. "What character did I act? My own?" he replied. "No; some unaccountable one. In short, I believe you have been trying to draw me out - or in; you have been talking nonsense to make me talk nonsense. It is scarcely fair, sir." "Do you forgive me, Jane?" "I cannot tell till I have thought it all over. If, on reflection, I find I have fallen into no great absurdity, I shall try to forgive you; but it was not right." "Oh! you have been very correct - very careful, very sensible."

Jane decided she had been quite sensible. At this moment she suddenly remembered that an unexpected guest had arrived. "His name is Mason, sir; and he comes from the West Indies; from Spanish Town, in Jamaica, I think." The effect of this news on Mr. Rochester startled Jane, for he gripped her wrist, caught his breath, turned white, and staggered, saying "I've got a blow, Jane … My little friend! I wish I were in a quiet island with only you; and trouble, danger, and hideous recollections removed from me." Jane got him a glass of wine and was relieved to see him rally and greet the mysterious guest cheerfully.

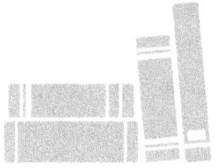

JANE EYRE

TEXTUAL ANALYSIS

CHAPTER 20

A strange night followed. As the moon shone bright and solemn into Jane's casement window, a terrible cry echoed from end to end of the house. Jane's pulse skipped; her heart stood still. Cries for help, for Mr. Rochester, could be heard, sounds of stamping, running, and crashing. In fright and confusion, some of the ladies sobbing, the guests poured into the cold hallway, just as Mr. Rochester came down from the third floor. He calmed his guests with a story of a servant's nightmare, and partly coaxed, partly ordered them to bed. Thinking he might need her, Jane dressed quietly. Sure enough he sent her for a sponge and smelling salts, and, making sure she would not faint at seeing blood, led her into a tapestried third floor bedroom. There lay the stranger Mason unconscious, his right side soaked with blood, while the mysterious laugh could be heard in the next room. Telling Jane she must alternately wipe the stranger's face and give him the salts and sips of water, Mr. Rochester rode off to fetch the surgeon. Much puzzled, Jane stayed at her post. What had brought Mason here? Why had his coming alarmed her master? Why was Mason now so tame and obedient? And what if the strange Fury next door should break out once more?

Just as streaks of dawn edged the sky, Mr. Rochester and the surgeon returned. Working swiftly, they bandaged the wounded man and dressed him in fresh clothes. Jane was still more puzzled by some of the things Mason said. "She bit me," he recalled, "she worried me like a tigress, when Mr. Rochester got the knife from her ... She sucked the blood: she said she'd drain my heart." Mr. Rochester urged him to take courage and forget the "gibberish" and finally managed to get Mason safely away in a postchaise.

Then, with relief, Mr. Rochester turned to Jane and suggested a walk in the grounds, saying that the house seemed like a dungeon. They strolled down a path with apple, pear, and peach trees on one side and a wealth of primroses, pansies, stocks, and briars on the other; "The sun was just entering the dappled east" and lit orchard and garden with morning sunshine. Jane was still apprehensive about Grace Poole, but to Mr. Rochester it was the thought of Mason which recalled his own situation. "To live, for me, Jane, is to stand on a crater-crust which may crack and spew fire any day." Mason, he said, might unwittingly harm him.

COMMENT

Again notice the care with which Charlotte provides a fresh, natural, and beautiful setting for a scene between Jane and Mr. Rochester.

Mr. Rochester asked Jane to sit with him on the garden bench, and it was apparent that he had a problem on his mind that he wanted to talk out with her. He asked if she thought someone who had committed a grave error (not a crime), an error from which he was still suffering, could take an unconventional means to avoid the consequences of his error. Clearly speaking of himself, Mr. Rochester admitted that in the past he had sought relief in "heartless, sensual pleasure," but claimed that recently he had been purified and renewed by the good and bright disposition of a new-found friend. "Is the wandering and sinful, but now rest-seeking and repentant man justified in daring the world's opinion, in order to attach to him forever this gentle, gracious, genial stranger; thereby securing his own peace of mind and regeneration of life?" Jane did not know what to say. She remarked that "a wanderer's repose or a sinner's reformation should never depend on a fellow-creature," and that Mr. Rochester should turn to God. Mr. Rochester cried mysteriously that God himself had provided the instrument of his reformation. But suddenly he broke off, his manner changed, and he asked Jane sarcastically if she did not think Blanche Ingram could regenerate him? With a complete return to his offhand, casual tone, he left Jane, calling to his guests, "Mason got the start of you all this morning ... I rose at four to see him off."

JANE EYRE

TEXTUAL ANALYSIS

CHAPTER 21

For about a week Jane dreamed almost every night of a small baby. This worried her because she remembered Bessie Leaven saying that "to dream of children was a sure sign of trouble." Sure enough, after a few days Bessie's husband, the coachman from Gateshead, arrived to tell her that John Reed had got into debt and killed himself and that Mrs. Reed had had a stroke and was asking for her. Reluctantly Mr. Rochester let her go; equally reluctantly Jane pointed out to him that if he did get married Adele ought to be sent away to school.

In two days Jane arrived at Gateshead and was greeted warmly by Bessie, coldly by Eliza and Georgiana. Indeed, she barely recognized the girls. Eliza was pale, severe, ascetic-looking, absorbed in an almost monastic private routine, while Georgiana was a plump, fashionable blond, hard-featured, superficial, and frivolous. They obviously had nothing in common, despised each other, and were not very concerned about their dying mother. Back in familiar, once-hated Gateshead, Jane took stock of herself and of the changes in her character since she had left there nearly nine years before. "...my prospects were doubtful yet; and I had yet an aching heart. I still felt as a wanderer on the face of the earth; but I experienced firmer trust in myself and my own powers, and less withering dread of oppression. The gaping wound of my wrongs, too, was now quite healed; and the flame of resentment extinguished." The realization of her growing maturity helped Jane not to shrink from her cousins' snubs and to face the interview with Mrs. Reed with poise. Actually when she saw her aunt lying helpless, she felt a rush of pity for her suffering and "a yearning to forget and forgive." Unfortunately, in her wanderings her aunt could only remember what an unnatural, rebellious child Jane was and how she hated her. It was some days before, with the fear of death over her, that she confessed the two wrongs she had done her. First, she had failed to bring her up as her own child, as she had promised her husband. Second, she had lied to Jane's uncle, John Eyre. Three years before he had written asking to have Jane sent to him in Madeira, where he would adopt her and leave her his fortune. "I could not forget your conduct to me, Jane - the fury with which you once turned on me; the tone in which you declared you abhorred me the worst of anybody in the world; the unchildlike look and voice with which you affirmed that ... I had treated you with miserable cruelty." "Dear Mrs. Reed," said Jane, "think no more of this, let it pass away from your mind. Forgive me for my passionate language: I was a child then; eight, nine years have passed since that day." "I tell you I could not forget it; and I took my revenge: for you to be adopted by your uncle, and placed in a state of ease and comfort, was what I could not endure. I wrote to him; I said I was sorry for his disappointment, but Jane Eyre was dead; she had died of typhus fever at Lowood. Now act as you please: write and contradict my assertion - expose my falsehood as soon as you like. You were born, I think, to be my torment..." Jane tried to persuade her aunt that she fully and freely forgave her and longed to be reconciled, but it was too late for Mrs. Reed to change such a deep-rooted hatred. She died late that night, hardly mourned even by Eliza and Georgiana.

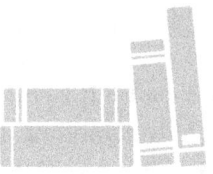

JANE EYRE

TEXTUAL ANALYSIS

CHAPTER 22

Jane stayed on to help Georgiana get off to London (where she later married a "wealthy worn-out man of fashion") and to look after the house while Eliza prepared to go to the Continent to become a nun. It was a month altogether before she took the hundred-mile, two-day trip back to Thornfield. At Millcote she left her box and set off to walk the few miles to Thornfield by a country road. It was a fair, soft summer evening; the hedges were full of roses, and the haymakers were at work as Jane neared the house. Unexpectedly, there was Mr. Rochester, sitting on the stile with a book and pencil in his hand. At seeing him again, Jane was shaken; her poise deserted her, and she trembled. Yet she "made shift to behave with decent composure."

"What the deuce have you done with yourself this last month?" I have been with my aunt, sir, who is dead." Mr. Rochester replied in his teasing way: "A true Janian reply! Good angels be my guard! She comes from the other world - from the abode of people who are dead; and tells me so when she meets me alone here in gloaming!" Quietly happy at being with him again, Jane is moved to an impulsive speech: "Thank you, Mr. Rochester, for your great kindness. I am strangely glad to get back again to you; and wherever you are is my home - my only home."

She walked quickly back to the house, where the household greeted her warmly. But as "a fortnight of dubious calm succeeded," Jane and Mrs. Fairfax were both puzzled that nothing was said of the master's marriage to Lady Blanche. He did not even ride to see her and passed off Mrs. Fairfax's inquiries with a joke. "I began," recalls Jane, "to cherish hopes I had no right to conceive: that the match was broken off... Never had he called me more frequently to his presence; never been kinder to me when there - and, alas! never had I loved him so well."

Comment

In Chapters 21 and 22, Charlotte Brontë paints a somewhat satirical portrait of an Anglo-Catholic (member of the High Church party in the Church of England). Anglo-Catholicism was an attempt on the part of John Henry Newman, John Keble, and others to restore to the Church of England much of what they thought beautiful in the worship of the medieval church and true in its theology and spiritual teachings. Newman took the further step of converting to the Church of Rome the year before Charlotte started *Jane Eyre*. Charlotte seems to have had no more sympathy with the Anglo-Catholic position than with the Evangelical one. Her portrait of Eliza is a caricature of an Anglo-Catholic.

JANE EYRE

TEXTUAL ANALYSIS

CHAPTER 23

It was an exceptionally beautiful summer. The hay was finished early, "the trees were in their dark prime" and contrasted sharply with the shorn meadows. On mid-summer-eve (i.e., the summer solstice, about June 21: it had supernatural associations) Jane wandered in the Edenlike seclusion of the orchard, watching a glorious sunset from near a big horse-chestnut tree. As the moon began to rise and a nightingale sang in the wood, Jane noticed in the air, as well as the fragrance of jasmine, rose, and sweetbriar, the scent of Mr. Rochester's cigar. A little shy, she tried to avoid meeting him, but he had seen her all along; and as a handsome moth alighted near him he said, "Jane, come and look at this fellow." They turned back to walk in the orchard, and Mr. Rochester talked of what was to happen to Jane when he was married to Miss Ingram. He was really only trying her out; but when he pretended he had found a place for her in Ireland, Jane began to cry quietly, because she would be so far away from him. When he told her to listen to the nightingale, she was overcome with emotion and sobbed convulsively. When she was able to speak, she made a sort of declaration: "I grieve to leave Thornfield: I love Thornfield: - I love it, because I have lived in it a full and delightful life - momentarily at least. I have not been trampled on. I have not been petrified. I have not been buried with inferior minds, and excluded from every glimpse of communion with what is bright and energetic, and high. I have talked, face to face, with what I reverence; with what I delight in, - with an original, a vigorous, an expanded mind. I have known you, Mr. Rochester; and it strikes me with terror and anguish to feel I absolutely must be torn from you forever." At this point Mr. Rochester dropped his pretense that he was marrying Blanche and proposed in earnest to Jane. Assuming he was mocking her, she replied full of indignation, "I have as much soul as you, - and full as much heart! And if God had gifted me with some beauty, and much wealth, I should have made it as hard for you to leave me, as it is now for me to leave you. I am not talking to you now through the medium of custom, conventionalities, or even of mortal flesh: - it is my spirit that addresses your spirit; just as if both had passed through the grave, and we stood at God's feet, equal, - as we are!" Finally Mr. Rochester was able to calm her and convince her that he really loved her and claimed her. They stayed out in the orchard, oblivious of a storm which was blowing up until the rain drove them indoors. In the morning, to Jane's astonishment, Adele told her that the great horse-chestnut tree had been rent in two by lightning.

COMMENT

Once more, notice the beauty and appropriateness of the setting; also the use of the storm to symbolize the emotional tumult within. Some critics think the destruction of the chestnut tree is a supernatural response to Rochester's sin in trying to marry Jane.

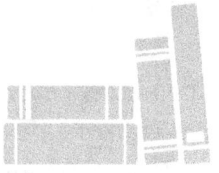

JANE EYRE

TEXTUAL ANALYSIS

CHAPTER 24

Next day, on a brilliant June morning, Jane looked into the glass and decided she did not look so plain as before; indeed Mr. Rochester commented that she looked "blooming, and smiling, and pretty." He drove her and Adele into Millcote and told the child that he was taking mademoiselle to the moon and invented other tales which emphasized Jane's elf-like nature. In the city he tried to buy her a quantity of silk dresses and jewels, but she would take only a "sober black satin and pearl-grey silk." She privately decided to write for money to her Uncle John in Madeira. It would be humiliating to be "kept" by Mr. Rochester indefinitely.

Meanwhile, she got Mr. Rochester to admit that his flirtation with Miss Ingram was intended to make her jealous. In the evenings she kept him from getting too sentimental by amusing him, talking back to him and getting him to sing. It was not, she says, always an easy task, but it was a delightful one. "My future husband was becoming to me my whole world; and more than the world: almost my hope of heaven. He stood between me and every thought of religion, as an eclipse intervenes between man and the broad sun. I could not, in those days, see God for his creature: of whom I had made an idol."

COMMENT

This passage is one of the clues to the moral and religious intention of the novel. Charlotte Brontë is preparing to show that Jane must put the claims of God and duty before her own happiness. This preparation begins as early as Chapter 14, where Jane and Rochester debate the nature of law.

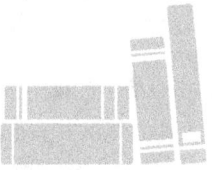

JANE EYRE

TEXTUAL ANALYSIS

CHAPTER 25

It was the day before the wedding and Jane's clothes and trunks were ready for the trip to Europe. She herself was anxious and restless. As she wandered in the orchard her mood was reflected in the stormy weather, the melancholy wail of the wind, and the momentary appearance of a blood-red moon. Mr. Rochester had been away, and Jane was relieved when she heard him galloping home. As they sat at supper by the fire she said, with a premonition of disaster. "I wish this present hour would never end: who knows with what fate the next may come charged?" She told him of two dreams which had troubled her sleep. The first was that she was walking with a little child in her arms and was unable to hurry, unable to catch up with her future husband. In the second dream she saw Thornfield Hall "a dreary ruin, the retreat of bats and elves." With the unknown child still clinging to her, in her dream Jane strove to climb the ruins, for she could see Mr. Rochester, "like a speak ... lessening every moment." Craving for a last look, Jane lost her balance, fell, and woke.

But these dreams were only a prelude to a terrifying event. Into her bedroom came a woman she had never seen before, "tall and large, with thick and dark hair hanging long down her back." Her face was discolored and savage, with red eyes and swollen lips. She looked like a vampire (a blood-sucking ghost). Taking down the beautiful wedding veil Mr. Rochester had bought for Jane, she first tried it on, then tore it in half and trampled on it. Then she stopped by the bedside and leaned over Jane, who was so frightened that she fainted. Mr. Rochester insisted that this must have been yet another nightmare, but Jane pointed out that the torn veil was there as evidence. At this Mr. Rochester was shaken, though he tried to persuade her that the apparition must have been Grace Poole. Nevertheless, he was alarmed enough to insist that Jane must sleep in the nursery with Adele and her nurse. He promised that after they were married a year and a day, he would explain why he kept Grace Poole on in his household. Somewhat comforted, Jane went to bed, but was too excited to sleep. "I ... waited for the coming day: all my life was awake and astir in my frame."

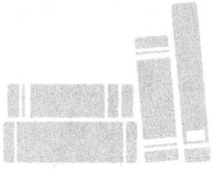

JANE EYRE

TEXTUAL ANALYSIS

CHAPTER 26

....

Next morning it was clear that Mr. Rochester was anxious to have the wedding over and to be off. He ordered the carriage, sent for Jane before she had finished dressing, and hurried her over to the church. As they paused for breath at the gate, Jane spied in the graveyard two strangers who later appeared in church, evidently wishing to witness the ceremony. As the bride and bridegroom knelt at the communion rail, the clergyman proceeded with the wedding service. All went smoothly until he reached the clause, "If either of you know any impediment why ye may not lawfully be joined together in matrimony, ye do now confess it." At this moment an extraordinary thing happened. One of the strangers stepped forward and said: "The marriage cannot go on: I declare the existence of an impediment." Mr. Rochester moved "as if an earthquake had rolled under his feet," but did not look around. The clergyman, at a loss, asked if the impediment might be overcome. "Hardly," replied the gentleman, "I have called it insuperable, and I speak advisedly ... It simply consists in the existence of a previous marriage. Mr. Rochester has a wife now living." Jane was thunderstruck; Mr. Rochester, his face colorless and his eyes glittering, put his arm around her. The stranger, who gave his name as Briggs, a lawyer from London, read an affidavit signed by Richard Mason. It affirmed that Edward Fairfax Rochester had been married to Mason's sister, Bertha Mason, at Spanish Town, Jamaica, fifteen years before. Mason now stepped forward to testify that he had seen his sister when he was at Thornfield in April. When Mr. Rochester heard this, after a long silence, he admitted the truth of Mason's statement. "Bigamy is an ugly word," he began, "I meant, however, to be a bigamist, but fate has out-manoeuvred me ... I have been married: and the woman to whom I was married lives ... I dare say," he went on to the clergyman, "you have inclined your ear to gossip about the mysterious lunatic kept there under watch and ward." The lunatic, he continued, was his wife, Bertha Mason, a madwoman and a drunkard, a member of a lunatic family. He had married in all innocence and had tried all these years to keep her existence a secret. Jane, he added, "knew nothing of this disgusting secret: she thought all was fair and legal ..." Ordering the coach away, he led the party to the third floor, where Grace Poole was cooking over the fire. There at the other end of the room, groveling on all fours, her shaggy locks hanging over her bloated face, was the fearful woman who had visited Jane's bedroom. She sprang for Mr. Rochester's throat; he grappled with her, finally pinioned her arms, and bound her with rope to a chair. Then he turned to his visitors. "That is my wife," he said. "Such is the sole conjugal embrace I am ever to know - such are the endearments which are to solace my leisure hours! And this [turning to Jane] is what I wished to have: this young girl, who stands so grave and quiet at the mouth of hell, looking collectedly at the gambols of a demon."

As they went down the stairs, the lawyer addressed Jane in words which gave her another surprise: "You madam," he said, "are clear from all blame: your uncle will be glad to hear it - if he should be still living - when Mr. Mason returns to Madeira." He explained that Jane's uncle, John Eyre, and Mr. Mason worked for the same firm, and that Mason had learned of the projected marriage from Mr. Eyre. The latter, much distressed at the deceit being practiced on his niece, but too ill to travel himself, had sent Mason to prevent the match. Still with a sense of shock, Jane locked herself into her bedroom to think. In a few hours her world had changed. Mr. Rochester had deceived her; perhaps then he did not truly love her. And "where was the Jane Eyre of yesterday? - Where was her life? - Where were her prospects?" She longed to be dead, "I came into deep waters; the floods overflowed me."

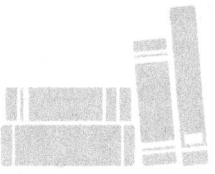

JANE EYRE

TEXTUAL ANALYSIS

CHAPTER 27

For hours Jane remained alone in her room, terrified at the solitude and suffering before her. She knew she must leave Thornfield. Finally, almost fainting from grief and hunger, she started into the hall, but fell-not on the ground, but into the arms of Mr. Rochester, who had been waiting by the door for her to come out. He was waiting to beg her forgiveness, which, when she saw his misery, she instantly gave. Downstairs, by the fireside, he told her the full story of his unhappy marriage. His father and elder brother Rowland had urged him into this marriage with the handsome daughter of a Jamaica planter for the sake of her dowry of thirty thousand pounds - a sum which would permit Rowland to inherit his father's estate intact. Mr. Rochester had been young and inexperienced at the time, had never seen Bertha alone, and was not aware (as his father and brother were) that there was insanity in the family, indeed that Bertha's mother and brother were already insane. Swayed by her beauty and her fortune, he married her. Four terrible years followed the marriage. Bertha proved to be coarse, ill-tempered, intemperate, and unchaste.

Eventually she was also pronounced mad, and Mr. Rochester, his life in ruins at twenty-six, almost fell into despair. His father and brother had died during this period, and the family estates were now his. It occurred to him that he might try to hide his lunatic wife at Thornfield. He brought her home, located Grace Poole to look after her, and himself travelled on the Continent, hoping to find someone he could really love, someone who would be willing if to marry him she understood the circumstances. Not finding such a woman, however, he took in succession three mistresses, though he admitted, in reply to Jane's shocked inquiry, that it was an unsatisfactory, "grovelling fashion of existence." Finally, "rid of all mistresses - in a harsh, bitter frame of mind … sourly disposed against all men, and especially against all womankind," he had come back to Thornfield on business, expecting no peace or pleasure there. But there, riding home on a frosty winter afternoon he had found, sitting quietly on a stile in the lane, the arbitress of his life, his "genius for good or evil" - Jane.

With deep feeling he described his growing delight in her - in her innocence, her good sense, and her shrewdness; in the contract between her shyness and diffidence on the one hand and her frankness and originality on the other. He saw that she had a wisdom of her own, a freshness of outlook and (in spite of her solitary life) "a social heart," one which responded with tenderness and friendship to his kindness. "After a youth and manhood passed half in unutterable misery and half in dreary solitude. I have for the first time found what I can truly love - I have found you. You are my sympathy - my better self - my good angel … " He begged her to be his, to go with him to a villa in the south of France where they could both be happy. It was a terrible moment for Jane. "Not a human being that ever lived could wish to be loved better than I was loved; and him who thus loved me I absolutely worshipped: and I must renounce love and idol." She made the difficult choice: "Mr. Rochester, I will not be yours." Nothing could move her from this decision. Mr. Rochester pictured the dreary solitude of his life without her, the possibility that he might fall again into vice, recklessness, or despair. Jane could not be shaken. "Do as I do," she counseled sadly, "trust in God and yourself. Believe in heaven. Hope to meet again there." There was no need to fall back into lust and vice. "We were born to strive and endure - you as well as I: do so." Once again she was tempted to give in. "Who in the world," she asked herself, "cares for you? or who will be injured by what you do?" Unanswerable was the reply, "I care for myself. The more solitary, the more friendless, the more unsustained I am, the more I will respect myself. I will keep the law given by God; sanctioned by man. I will hold to the principles received by me when I was sane, and not mad - as I am now." Physically, she knew she was weak, "powerless as stubble exposed to the drought and glow of a furnace," but she told herself "mentally, I still possessed my soul." In spite of Mr. Rochester's anguish - and her own - she bade him farewell.

That night Jane dreamed that she was a child again, alone and unprotected. But to counter that dream, she had a vision of her mother, whose spirit spoke to her spirit: "My daughter, flee temptation!" "Mother, I will." Making up a parcel of a few clothes, some bread, and twenty shillings, Jane stole out of the house just as dawn was breaking. On the highway she stopped the coach and paid the fare to a distant town.

COMMENT

Jane has at last learned part of the lesson which Helen Burns tried to teach her; she has learned to do right whatever it may cost, to suffer what has to be suffered. She has developed her own individual religion, based on belief in God, in conscience, and in her own personal integrity.

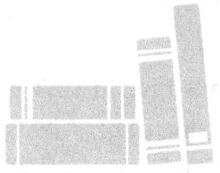

JANE EYRE

TEXTUAL ANALYSIS

CHAPTER 28

After two days' travel the coachman set Jane down at a crossroads near the village of Morton (identified as Hathersage in Derbyshire). In her disturbed state she forgot her parcel and so had no bread or extra clothes. She lay on the heath that night, feeling that Nature at least had not cast her off. Her heart still trembling for Mr. Rochester, Jane rose to her knees to pray. "Night has come, and her planets were risen: a safe, still night; too serene for the companionship of fear. We know that God is everywhere; but certainly we feel His presence most when His works are on the grandest scale spread before us ... Looking up, I, with tear-dimmed eyes, saw the mighty Milky-way ... I felt the might and strength of God ... I turned my prayer to thanksgiving: the Source of Life was also the Saviour of spirits. Mr. Rochester was safe: he was God's and by God he would be guarded." When Jane got up in the morning, she wished that God had called her to Himself in the night. "Life, however, was yet in my possession: with all its requirements, and pains, and responsibilities. The burden must be carried; the want provided for; the suffering endured; the responsibility fulfilled."

COMMENT

The two passages just quoted probably represent part of Charlotte's own creed. Love and life are both under God; but the loss of love does not absolve one from the responsibilities of living life.

The rest of the day Jane wandered about the village, trying to find work as a seamstress or servant, trying to exchange her scarf or gloves for bread. Often rebuffed, she realized that her problems were her own, that she had no claim on these people. Eventually, however, hunger forced her to beg some bread and some porridge intended for a pig. Toward night she strayed toward the heath again, soaked with the rain which was by then falling heavily. Seeing a light on the edge of the moor, she somewhat hopelessly made her way toward it, coming at last to a long, low house overgrown with some creeping plant. Through the latticed windows she could see a clear, plain room, an elderly servant knitting, and two girls in mourning, apparently engaged in translating German. Jane gathered from what she overheard that their father had recently died and that they were expecting their brother shortly. The girls seemed refined, and as they were her last hope, Jane plucked up her courage to knock and ask to see them. The servant turned her away, and at last Jane broke down and wept. "I believe in God," she cried aloud. "Let me try to wait His will in silence." At that moment the brother returned and caught the last few sentences. Something about Jane's voice or aspect must have intrigued him, for he bade her go into the house, where she stood sick and trembling, conscious of her bedraggled appearance. St. John (the brother; pronounced "sinjun") told one sister to give Jane some bread dipped in milk. He tried to elicit some facts about Jane, but she was too exhausted to do more than give him an alias, "Jane Elliott." "Hannah," said St. John to the servant, "let her sit here at present, and ask her no questions; in ten minutes more, give her the remainder of that milk and bread. Mary and Diana, let us go into the parlour and talk the matter over." The result of the family conference was happy for Jane. "My dripping clothes were removed; soon, a warm, dry bed received me. I thanked God-experienced amidst unutterable exhaustion a glow of grateful joy - and slept."

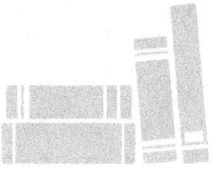

JANE EYRE

TEXTUAL ANALYSIS

CHAPTER 29

....

Jane was very ill for three days from nervous strain and fatigue. On the third day she was able to eat a little and struggle downstairs to the kitchen where she made friends with Hannah, who she felt had resented her presence. As they picked over gooseberries, Jane learned from Hannah that the three young people were the last of the Rivers, and old and respected family of the neighborhood. The three were very close and took after their mother in their love of learning. At this moment the family returned and, happy to find Jane better, invited her into the parlor. Again St. John asked Jane about her past and her connections, but again she answered evasively, telling him only that she was a clergyman's daughter, educated at Lowood School, and a governess. She did admit that the name she had given them was an alias. She declared herself anxious to find work, willing to do anything however humble. St. John said that if this were true he would be very willing to help her, so far as he was able to.

JANE EYRE

TEXTUAL ANALYSIS

CHAPTER 30

Jane found the Rivers girls companionable. When the weather was fine, she enjoyed walking with them to the little wild pastures with their flocks of moorland sheep or on the purple sweeps of moorland with their tiny flowers and granite crags. Indoors the girls were equally companionable, discussing books and ideas and learning German together. Jane's ability in drawing, superior to theirs, surprised and charmed them. St. John, more reserved and absorbed in his work, was less friendly. Finally, though, Jane reminded him that he had promised to help her find work. He replied coolly and mysteriously that the work had been ready for three weeks. After speaking a little of his own future as a missionary, he finally told Jane that he would provide her with a small cottage if she would be willing to be the teacher of a school for the village children which he proposed to open - a humble and narrow task, but one which would give her the independence she needed, for Diana and Mary would shortly have to return to their positions in the city. "I thank you for the proposal, Mr. Rivers," said Jane. "I accept it with all my heart." St. John was still dubious, though pleased at her willingness. "I am sure you cannot long be content to pass your leisure in solitude, and to devote your working hours to a monotonous labour wholly void of stimulus; any more than I can be content," he added, with emphasis "to live here buried in morass, pent in with mountains - my nature, that God gave me, contravened; my faculties, heaven-bestowed, paralysed - made useless." After this outburst, which rather astonished Jane, he disappeared. Later he returned reading a letter. "Our Uncle John is dead," he told the girls, who explained to Jane that this unknown uncle, their mother's brother, once gave their father bad advice over speculations, as a consequence of which he lost most of his money. Later the uncle became prosperous, and they had been rather hoping he might leave them something. Now it appeared he had left about twenty thousand pounds, the bulk of his fortune, not to them, but to another relative.

COMMENT

When Charlotte wrote of the pleasures of sharing intellectual and other enjoyments, she was probably thinking of her own close relationship with her sisters.

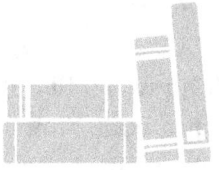

JANE EYRE

TEXTUAL ANALYSIS

CHAPTER 31

Jane was soon installed in her tiny two-room cottage and held her first class. She was a little discouraged to find that only three of her twenty pupils could read and that none could write or figure. She was dismayed by their ignorance, coarseness, and poverty, but reminded herself that they were human beings and that she must strive to develop whatever germs of refinement, intelligence, and good feeling they might have. She also had to struggle with her grief over Mr. Rochester, and at the end of the day she found herself in tears. St. John came at this point with a present of paints, pencils, and drawing paper from his sisters, who had left for the city. Seeing Jane's face, he was afraid she was disappointed in her cottage or her pupils, but she reassured him, saying she was content and thankful. St. John advised her not to look to the past, but to pursue her present task for a season. He said he knew from experience how hard it was to work contrary to one's natural bent, but that it could and should be done. "God has given us, in a measure, the power to make our own fate." He spoke again of his longing to become a missionary, of his determination to break through any entanglement of his feelings any human weakness which might prevent his going.

At this moment a young, graceful, and very lovely girl came up the path. She was Rosamund Oliver, the daughter of a local manufacturer. It was she who had endowed the school, furnished the cottage, and chosen a little orphan who was to be Jane's servant. She would come and help teach, too, she said. When she spoke of going to a dance, St. John seemed disturbed, for he looked at her with "an unsmiling, a searching, a meaning gaze." He did not respond to her friendly chatter and refused an invitation to visit her father that evening. The refusal evidently cost him an effort, for his face was white. "This spectacle of another's suffering and sacrifice," recalls Jane, "rapt my thoughts from exclusive meditation on my own. Diana Rivers had designated her brother 'inexorable as death.' She had not exaggerated."

JANE EYRE

TEXTUAL ANALYSIS

CHAPTER 32

At first Jane found her village school hard work and her scholars all "hopelessly dull." However, she soon found that "there was a difference amongst them as amongst the educated" and that the more able among them soon improved in neatness and good manners and in their studies. Jane herself began to take pleasure in their progress and in getting acquainted with their families.

Behind the facade of tranquility, however, Jane still suffered much anguish at the loss of Mr. Rochester. She dreamed of him often, "dreams many-colored, agitated," dreams of "loving him and being loved by him." Meantime she could not help noticing the attraction between St. John and Rosamund Oliver, an attraction which he seemed bent on resisting, although Rosamund's interest in him was quite apparent. She came often to school, usually when St. John was teaching the catechism. Jane thought it was a pity that St. John cared too much about his reward in heaven to marry this lovely girl, for she had many good qualities and with her money St. John could do a great deal of good. After making sure that Rosamund's father would raise no objection, she tackled St. John on the subject, drawing his attention to a portrait of Rosamund she was working on. He admitted to loving her but denied that she would be a suitable wife for him. "... To twelve months' rapture would succeed a lifetime or regret ... While something in me," he went on, "is acutely sensible to her charms, something else is as deeply impressed with her defects: they are such that she could sympathize in nothing I aspired to - co-operate in nothing I undertook. Rosamund a sufferer, a labourer, a female apostle? Rosamund a missionary's wife? No!" And he repudiated with passion Jane's proposal to give up his vocation. He would not even accept her offer to paint for him a copy of the portrait of Rosamund. But as he was looking at Jane's papers, he suddenly snatched up one piece, tore a bit from the edge, and vanished, leaving Jane much astonished.

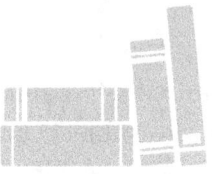

JANE EYRE

TEXTUAL ANALYSIS

CHAPTER 33

The next evening St. John returned in a strange mood. After sitting in silence for some time, he began to tell Jane a tale of an orphan whose aunt sent her to a charity school and who became governess to a ward of a certain Mr. Rochester. Too surprised to protest, Jane wanted most to hear news of Mr. Rochester, but St. John was more concerned with other aspects of the story. He had inquiries from Briggs, the London lawyer, for a "Jane Eyre" but only recognized her as the "Jane Elliott" of his school when she inadvertently scribbled her own name on one of her papers. That was what he had so hastily torn off the day before.

But there was more to the story than his identification of Jane Eyre with Jane Elliott. The "Uncle John" who had died turned out to be not only the Rivers' uncle but also Jane's uncle, the John Eyre of Madeira who had inquired about her at Gateshead. Before he died he had made a will bequeathing a fortune of twenty thousand pounds to - his niece Jane Eyre! Jane was so excited she could hardly breathe. She was even more delighted with three new cousins than with her fortune, which, indeed, she insisted on dividing with them, so that they should have five thousand pounds apiece.

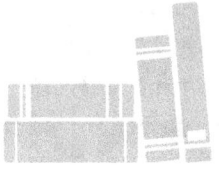

JANE EYRE

TEXTUAL ANALYSIS

CHAPTER 34

Joyfully Jane said goodbye to her scholars and with Hannah's help prepared Moore House in readiness for the home-coming of Mary and Diana, who could now afford to leave their work in the city. Together, Jane and Hannah polished the woodwork until it shone, lit fires in all the rooms, and baked cakes and mince pies for Christmas. Jane's spirits were a little dashed because St. John took no interest in these preparations, but instead reminded her of the parable of the talents (Matthew 25: 14–30) and hoped she would "look a little higher than domestic endearments and household joys." He himself pursued his parish duties with relentless and sacrificial zeal. Shortly after Mary and Diana returned, St. John told them that Rosamund Oliver was engaged to someone else; to Jane he remarked, "The battle is fought and the victory won" - meaning that his ambition to be a missionary had been victorious over his desire for Rosamund. At this point he persuaded Jane to study "Hindostanee" (an Indian language) with him. He proved a patient but very exacting teacher, and

Jane found that day by day she strained every nerve to satisfy and please him. After some time he tried to persuade Jane to marry him and accompany him to India. Jane protested that she had no vocation, no taste for missionary life. In reply St. John argued that she had run the village school with ability and tact, dealt with her legacy without greed or selfishness, studied a strange language with perseverance to please him and, in short, was "diligent, disinterested, faithful, constant, and courageous; very gentle and very heroic."

COMMENT

Notice how Charlotte uses this opportunity to comment on Jane's moral and spiritual development.

Jane pondered the proposal for some time. She had heard no word from Mr. Rochester; even Mrs. Fairfax did not answer her letters. England without Mr. Rochester was an empty land, and at least the life of a missionary was a noble one. But the idea of marrying without love was repugnant to her. She recognized that St. John saw in her only a competent colleague, a good weapon, a useful tool. She told him she was willing to go as a companion, but not as a wife. He argued that to take such a young female companion would violate the proprieties. Jane insisted that all she could give was "a comrade's constancy" - which was, in fact, exactly what St. John wanted - a loyalty he could use and mound to his purposes. Inwardly, he was annoyed that Jane did not fall in with his plans; outwardly, he maintained a cold politeness which hurt her more than if he had hit her.

JANE EYRE

TEXTUAL ANALYSIS

CHAPTER 35

Jane made one attempt at a reconciliation with St. John, for she valued his friendship; but he merely repeated his demand that she come to India as his wife. When the household met for prayers that night, he read a passage from the New Testament which concluded: "He that overcometh shall inherit all things; and I will be his God, and he shall be my son. But the fearful, the unbelieving, etc. shall have their part in the lake which burneth with fire and brimstone, which is the second death [Revelation 21: 7–8]." As he bade her farewell before setting out for Cambridge, he begged her once more to "repent" and go with him. This time he spoke gently and Jane was much moved. "The Impossible ... was fast becoming the Possible ... Religion called - Angels beckoned - God commanded - life rolled together like a scroll - death's gates opening, showed eternity beyond: it seemed, that for safety and bliss there, all here might be sacrificed in a second." But just as she was about to give in, a strange "inexpressible feeling," sharp as an electric shock, came over her. Clearly she heard her name called by a familiar, "loved, well-remembered voice - that of Edward Fairfax Rochester; and it spoke in pain and woe wildly, eerily, urgently." "I am coming," she called in answer. "Wait for me! Oh, I will come!" Bidding St. John to leave her, she knelt in prayer. "I seemed to penetrate very near a Mighty Spirit; and my soul rushed out in gratitude at His feet. I rose from the thanksgiving - took a resolve - and lay down, unscared, enlightened - eager for the daylight."

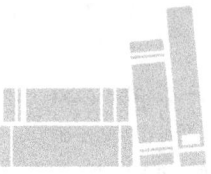

JANE EYRE

TEXTUAL ANALYSIS

CHAPTER 36

Next morning, June first, Jane was up at dawn. St. John had left her a note saying, "Watch and pray, that you enter not into temptation." He said that if Jane had stayed longer, she would have laid her "hand on the Christian's cross." After he set out for Cambridge, Jane took the coach for Millcote and got off at the Rochester Arms near Thornfield. It was exactly a year since she had left it. In the greatest excitement she hurried past the stile and through the fields toward the hall, hoping to see Mr. Rochester at his window or in the orchard. A shock was in store for her. The house was "a blackened ruin." The front was merely a shell, as she had once seen it in a dream (Ch. 25); roof, battlement, and chimney were gone. Signs of a fire were everywhere, and a deathlike silence reigned. Returning to the inn, Jane forced herself to ask the innkeeper what had happened at Thornfield. She dreaded to hear bad news of Mr. Rochester.

Her garrulous informer kept her in suspense, for he dwelt at some length on Mr. Rochester's infatuation for the governess, his attempt to marry her, and his search for her after she ran away. At last, however, the host came back to the story of the fire. The madwoman had eluded Grace Poole's care, set fire to a room on the third floor, and gone down to the governess's room and set the bed there alight. Soon the whole house was in flames. Mr. Rochester had helped all the servants out and gone back up for his wife when all those watching saw her on the roof, waving her arms, her hair streaming black against the flames. As Mr. Rochester called to her, she threw herself down and was killed.

COMMENT

The description of Bertha Mason's death is reminiscent of the death of Ulrica in Scott's *Ivanhoe*. Evidently this dramatic scene lingered long in Charlotte's memory.

Rochester himself was badly hurt. As he was coming down the staircase, the ruins fell in and he was buried. He was pulled out, but one eye was destroyed and one hand so crushed that it had to be amputated. The sight of the other eye had since gone, and Mr. Rochester was living in isolation at the manor of Ferndean, looked after by two servants. Jane immediately hired a post chaise and set off for Ferndean.

JANE EYRE

TEXTUAL ANALYSIS

CHAPTER 37

Ferndean proved to be a rather ancient house in the midst of a gloomy wood. Jane arrived at dusk. A figure came out into the twilight. It was Mr. Rochester, his hand outstretched to see if it was raining, his face "desperate and brooding." Jane spoke to John and Mary, the servants, and when Mr. Rochester asked for a glass of water, took it in herself. She was so nervous she spilled half of it. "Will you have a little more water, sir?" she asked. "Who is it? Who speaks?" he demanded, and at first he thought her voice was a delusion. Then he reached for her hand and embraced her. "Is it Jane?" he asked again. "This is her shape - this is her size - " "And this is her voice," Jane answered, "She is all here: her heart, too. God bless you, sir! I am glad to be so near you again." It was a happy reunion. Jane felt both excited and at ease with Mr. Rochester: "All I said or did seemed either to console or revive him. Delightful consciousness! It brought to life and light my whole nature: in his presence I thoroughly lived; and he lived in mine.'" Jane had much to tell him - about her school-teaching, about her legacy, about her newfound cousins. She managed to make him rather jealous of St. John, which she hoped would jolt him out of his melancholy. At last he brought up the subject of marriage. "Choose," said Jane, "her who loves you best." "Her I love best," he replied, and asked Jane if he suited her. Her reply was heartfelt: "To the finest fibre of my nature, sir."

Rochester, too, had things to tell her of the time since they had seen each other. His experience in suffering had brought him closer to God. He had begun to pray as he had not prayed for years. Now he felt profoundly thankful to God, who had finally given him happiness out of so much misery. He also told Jane of a strange thing which had happened four days before. "I was in my own room," he recounted, "and sitting by the window, which was open: it soothed me to feel the balmy night-air; though I could see no stars, and only by vague, luminous haze, knew the presence of a moon. I longed for thee, Jane! Oh, I longed for thee both with soul and flesh! ... and the alpha and omega of my heart's wishes broke involuntarily from my lips in the words - 'Jane! Jane! Jane!'" He thought he heard an answer "I am coming: wait for me." This had happened the very day and hour when Jane had heard the mysterious voice in the night.

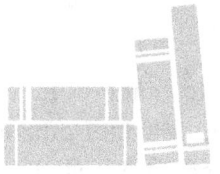

JANE EYRE

TEXTUAL ANALYSIS

CHAPTER 38

....

Three days later Jane and Mr. Rochester were married. Diana and Mary wrote warmly when they heard the news; St. John did not answer at the time, and when he did write he made no reference to Jane's marriage, but reminded her to keep her heart on heavenly things. Meanwhile Jane had visited Adele, found her unhappy in a very strict school, and brought her home until she found a more suitable school. "As she grew up, a sound English education corrected in a great measure her French defects."

Jane was deeply happy in her marriage. "No woman was ever nearer to her mate than I am: ever more absolutely bone of his bone, and flesh of his flesh. I know no weariness of my Edward's society: he knows none of mine, any more than we each do of the pulsation of the heart that beats in our separate bosoms; consequently, we are ever together. To be together is for us to be at once as free as in solitude, as gay as in company. We talk, I believe, all day long: to talk to each other is but a more animated and an audible thinking." Eventually Mr. Rochester recovered his sight somewhat. "When his first-born was put into his arms, he could see that the boy had inherited his own eyes, as they once were - large, brilliant, and black."

Diana and Mary Rivers both married happily and kept up their friendship with Jane. St. John did not marry, but went to India where he labored as a missionary with energy, zeal, and self-denial. His last letter hinted that his death was near and that he would meet it unafraid saying, "Amen; even so come, Lord Jesus."

JANE EYRE

TEXTUAL ANALYSIS

CONCLUSION

To repeat, *Jane Eyre* is an intensely personal book. It is not a historical novel; it is not a satirical novel; it does not mirror society; it does not have a social message. As Mrs. Tillotson says, "it maps a private world. Private, but not eccentric. *Jane Eyre* is now read by thousands who have no idea of its period, many of them too young or too unsophisticated for clear discrimination of past from present, imaginary from actual; who devour it, unaware of difficulties, unconscious of any need for adaptation to unfamiliar manners or conventions. And this is a part, perhaps the vital part, of the response of all its readers" (p. 257). Cecil, too, remarks on the timelessness which is part of the perennial appeal of the book. "Gone is the busy prosaic urban world with its complicated structure and its trivial motives, silenced the accents of everyday chatter, vanished are newspapers, fashions, business houses, duchesses, footmen and snobs. Instead the gale rages under the elemental sky, while indoors, their faces rugged in the fierce firelight, austere figures of no clearly defined class or period declare eternal love and hate to one another in phrases of stilted eloquence and staggering candour" - (p. 100). He notes, too (pp. 143-135) the difficulty of ranking Charlotte with other novelists. She is too faulty to be ranked with the very greatest writers, a Shakespeare or a Jane Austen, but neither can she be considered a minor figure. "She is predestined to hover restlessly and forever, now at the head now at the foot of the procession of letters, among the unplaceable anomalies, the freak geniuses; along with Ford and Tourneur and Herman Melville and D. H. Lawrence. Such writers never achieve a universally accepted reputation. The considerable body of people who set a paramount importance on craftsmanship and verisimilitude will never admire them. But their strange flame, lit as it is at the central white hot fire of creative inspiration, will in every age find them followers. And on these they exercise a unique, a thrilling, a perennial fascination."

JANE EYRE

CHARACTER ANALYSES

THE CHARACTER OF JANE AND THE MEANING OF THE NOVEL

What gives the scenes and events of *Jane Eyre* conviction is the vitality of the teller. Everything is seen through the eyes of Jane herself, and she is intensely real. According to McCullogh (p. 170), this is what was new in *Jane Eyre*. "The real innovation of Charlotte Brontë is that she writes fiction from the point of view of an individual and not from the point of view of society in general. She projects herself without reserve into her leading characters and allows her inmost feelings, her secret impulses, to color her narrative …" Her aim was not simply to provoke sympathy for her heroine but rather to express or realize her … She was, like Wordsworth, possessed by her feelings as well as possessing them … She did not attempt to get at the sources of behavior but simply to present it. What is vital in her work will not quickly perish because it deals with life in terms which do not generally change" (p. 173). Charlotte was also presenting through the character of Jane some of her own most deeply felt convictions, convictions of permanent importance in human life - the right of the humblest person to affection and self-realization, honesty and integrity, the right to speak out frankly, and the claims of morality and religion. The inner story of the novel, much more important than the melodramatic plot on which it hangs, is the story of Jane's long struggle to attain these values, to become a person who is admired, respected, and cared for, without compromising any of her other principles.

GATESHEAD AND LOWOOD

The struggle has already begun for the despised, outcast, unprotected child at the Reeds. At this stage Jane's instinct for self-assertion can only express itself in rebellion. Goaded by John Reed's bullying, she hits back on two occasions, fighting like a mad cat until she is overpowered. Stung by Mrs. Reed's accusations that she is deceitful, she hits back in words, insisting on her own honesty, telling her aunt how much she dislikes her and making her first articulate claim for love: "You think I have no feelings and that I can do without one bit of love or kindness; but I cannot live so ..." Terror as well as anger runs away with her feelings when she is locked in the red-room where her own vivid imagination frightens her into a kind of fit. Yet in her soberer moments she can be realistic and objective enough to see that she is "a discord at Gateshead," to understand why her personality does not appeal to her aunt, to realize that she is not heroic enough to go and live with poor relatives. At this stage, her ideas about religion are naive in the extreme. But at Lowood she comes face to face with real humility and genuine religious faith in the person of Helen Burns. Jane cannot accept the idea of humility. When Helen reminds her that the Bible tells us to return good for evil, Jane disagrees, insisting that we must "strike back very hard," resist injustice, return dislike with dislike. She listens in wonder as Helen urges her not to waste time or energy in hatred, but to endure suffering patiently and to prepare for eternity. At this point Jane cannot accept most of these ideas, but she has learned one lesson from Helen. Though she suffers from shame and anger when punished before the whole school, she does try to endure her punishment stoically. But she still craves affection: "If others don't love me, I would rather die than live." Helen's reply: "You think too much of the love of human beings," finds echoes much later in the book, when Jane admits to loving Rochester to the point of idolatry. Helen's dying declaration of faith impresses Jane but does not convince her - she can only ask " Where is God? What is God?"

THORNFIELD

By the time she leaves Lowood, eight years later, Jane has learned "an allegiance to duty and order," but her longing for excitement and fulfillment is not satisfied. Her restlessness drives her to seek a new position, but at first her life as a governess at Thornfield does not satisfy her either, and she notes with indignation that women want more out of life than housework and embroidery. But the return of Mr. Rochester completely transforms her life. His attention to her delights her. His questions about her history, his comments on her pictures, his confidences about his past feed her vanity and challenge her intelligence and wit. His eccentric manners only put her at ease. His teasing enchants her. She grieves for his secret grief, rejoices when she is able to save him from the fire, and is deeply moved when he thanks her for this ("billows of trouble rolled under surges of joy"). Though not unaware that she loves him, she tries to keep her feet on the ground and remind herself that she is a poor, plain governess - especially after Mrs. Fairfax tells her about the beautiful Blanche Ingram. When Rochester leaves her alone with the injured Mason, she shows that she can act with courage and discretion. Her return to Gateshead to see her dying aunt reminds us how much she has grown in the years since she left there, and gives her an opportunity to take stock of herself. "I still felt as a wanderer on the face of the earth; but I experienced a firmer trust in myself and my own powers, and less withering dread of oppression." She bears the snubs of her cousins with a new equanimity, and pities her helpless aunt with all her heart. She has learned to forgive.

Jane needs all the maturity she can muster, for when she returns to Thornfield she has to undergo a testing which will try her strength and spirit to the utmost. When Rochester answers her claim to equality of soul with him (Chap. 23) by affirming it and proposing to her, she is blissfully happy and seems on the brink of the fulfillment for which she longed. But looking back she realizes that she had not yet learned the lesson Helen Burns tried to teach, "You think too much of the love of human beings." "My future husband was becoming to me my whole world; and more than the world; almost my hope of heaven. He stood between me and every thought of religion, as an eclipse intervenes between man and the broad sun. I could not, in those days, see God for his creature: of whom I had made an idol." She must be tested further and learn to serve God first.

The test comes when the identity of Bertha Mason is revealed and Rochester begs Jane to go away with him. Jane knows that this would be wrong, but the decision is a terrible one, and this great Temptation Scene in Chapter 27 is the heart of the novel. Everything is done to make it hard for her to refuse him - her own love, deeper than ever, his repentance for deceiving her, his manly appeal for forgiveness, his moving account of his wrongs and vicissitudes, his insistence that she is the agent of his regeneration and that without her he may fall back into vice and depravity. Jane reflects that she may "drive a fellow-creature to despair," and asks herself, "Who in the world cares for you? or who will be injured by what you do?" The answer is inexorable: "I care for myself. The more solitary, the more friendless, the more unsustained I am, the more I will respect myself. I will keep the law given by God; sanctioned by man." She reminds Mr. Rochester: "We were born to strive and endure." And in the hour of her temptation she responds to the "invisible world" of which Helen Burns spoke so long ago. Her soul is her own, and when her mother's spirit tells her to "flee temptation," she responds by doing what she has to do - leaving Thornfield and Mr. Rochester behind - "God must have led me on."

MOOR HOUSE AND FERNDEAN

In the long interlude before Jane is reunited with Mr. Rochester, she is tested still further, but she has grown in moral power and in recognition that she is fully responsible for what she is and does. When hunger assails her, she realizes that it is her problem, not that of strangers. When work is offered her, she accepts it and does it well, silently battling her grief for Mr. Rochester. When money is left to her, she handles it without greed or injustice. Then comes the proposal from St. John Rivers that she marry him and become a missionary. It is a temptation contrary to the one Rochester offered. He tempted her to pleasure, love, and passion but without morality. St. John tempts her to a life of self-sacrifice, duty, and usefulness, but without love. Jane instinctively feels that marriage without love is prostitution, but she is aware how powerful this second temptation is - almost as powerful as Rochester's especially when St. John speaks gently and tenderly to her. This second time, too, she very nearly gives in. "Religion called - Angels beckoned - God commanded - life rolled together like a scroll - death's gates opening, showed eternity beyond: it seemed, that for safety and bliss there, all here might be sacrificed in a second. The dim room was full of visions." This time she is saved, not by her own conscience, but by the mysterious voice calling her name. In her return to Thornfield and her search for Rochester, the story moves toward a conventional joyful conclusion, but Jane's happiness has been earned. Without violating her integrity or her conscience, Jane's struggle for self-realization and her longing for love and fulfillment are both realized. "There was no harassing restraint, no repressing of glee and vivacity; for with him I was at perfect ease ... Delightful consciousness! It brought to life and light my whole nature: in his presence I thoroughly lived." "Jane suits me: do I suit her?" he asks. "To the finest fibre of my nature, sir." The "finest fibre" is moral and spiritual as well as emotional. Jane's achievement of it is the meaning of the book.

EDWARD FAIRFAX ROCHESTER

Rochester's character is only gradually revealed to Jane and to the reader. He is made to sound rather enigmatic even before he appears. Mrs. Fairfax finds it hard to characterize him and can only say that he is a gentleman, but peculiar in that one never knows whether he is in jest or in earnest. He has not the conventional good looks of a hero, for he is dark, stern, and rather ugly. He does not act the conventional master with Jane, either. On the first night he is asking her if she belongs to the men in green (elves) and pretending she bewitched his horse, to the complete mystification of Mrs. Fairfax; soon he is examining her paintings with some penetration ("who taught you to paint wind?") and much curiosity. Yet in spite of his obvious interest in her, he is very changeable, sometimes leaving her abruptly almost in the midst of a conversation, sometimes staring with strange looks at the battlements. His account of his relationship with Adele's mother does not reflect credit on his morals, but his desire to be a better man than he has been is in his favor. Jane writes that he is "proud, sardonic, harsh to inferiority of every description" and wonders at his occasional moods of savage gloom and anger. When Mason is hurt, he shows that he can keep his head and act with authority and dispatch, yet he tells Jane gloomily that he is standing "on a crater-crust which may crack and spew fire any day." His sudden changes of mood and abrupt departures continue.

His strange behavior is accounted for in the ensuing chapters when the existence of Bertha Mason is revealed. He has evidently been making up his mind whether he dare marry Jane and perhaps whether he can without hurting her. Meanwhile in his wooing of Jane he displays other qualities - his teasing which emphasizes Jane's other-worldly qualities, his rare, special smile which so charms her, his feeling for the beauty of the natural world, his characteristic desire to test Jane to drive her to acknowledgment of her feelings, his enjoyment of her wit and originality. Most remarkable is his response to her claim to equality of souls - "It is my spirit that addresses your spirit; just as if both had passed through the grave, and we stood at God's feet, equal, - as we are!" He acknowledges that they are indeed equal and that their souls are alike (Chap. 23). (This belief in the mutual attraction of like souls was common to both Charlotte and Emily Brontë. Readers of *Wuthering Heights* will remember Cathy's expression of this doctrine in Chap. 9.)

We see nothing of Mr. Rochester during the year of Jane's absence, but we hear from the innkeeper of his long anxious search for Jane and of his heroism in the fire. But it is Rochester himself who tells us of the change which has come over him in his desolation. In the face of complete disaster, his proud spirit has been humbled and he has turned to God: "I began to experience remorse, repentance; the wish for reconcilement to my Maker. I began sometimes to pray: very brief prayers they were, but very sincere." It is after the most heartfelt of these prayers that

Rochester utters his cry to Jane and hears her voice reply. Reunited with Jane, he prays that he may have strength to lead a purer life.

Readers of *Jane Eyre* have differed greatly as to whether they have found Rochester convincing or unconvincing. "No flesh-and-blood man could be so exclusively composed of violence and virility and masculine vanity as Mr. Rochester," writes Cecil (p. 115). He thinks that Charlotte "felt far too remote from that unaccountable wild animal called man to try to get inside him" (p. 114). He recognizes, of course, that Rochester is seen strictly from the narrator's viewpoint. "But if we had a chance to see Mr. Rochester with our own eyes - it is a solemn thought - he would certainly have looked different from what he does when seen through the eyes of Jane Eyre" (p. 104). Virginia Woolf (p. 110), too, observes that "the portrait of Rochester is drawn in the dark." Allen (pp. 115, 118) speaks of him as a "symbol of virility," another master figure in the master-pupil relationship which Charlotte found so appealing, a symbol of a figure over which Jane triumphs, in that at the end of the novel she is stronger than the helpless Rochester. On the other hand, McCullogh (p. 181) views Rochester as a serious character who undergoes a several moral "struggle between his love and desire and his fear of wronging her [Jane]," which accounts for his peculiar behavior. Moreover, Phyllis Bentley (*The Brontës*, p. 67) claims that Rochester "is saved from being a mere hero of melodrama by his very real wit, pride, intelligence and ugliness." The reader will have to make up his own mind after reading the novel. Meanwhile, it is interesting to read how Charlotte herself envisioned her hero. She describes him in a letter to her publisher's reader: "Mr. Rochester has a thoughtful nature and a very feeling heart; he is neither selfish nor self-indulgent; he is ill-educated, misguided; errs, when he does err, through rashness and inexperience: he lives for a time as too many other men live, but being radically better than most men, he does not like that degraded life, and is never happy in it. He is taught the severe lessons of experience and has sense to learn wisdom from them. Years improve him; the effervescence of youth foamed away, what is really good in him still remains. His nature is like wine of a good vintage, time cannot sour, but only mellows him. Such at least was the character I meant to portray."

MINOR CHARACTERS

Charlotte Brontë's characters are shown through action and dialogue. Her comments on them, through Jane, are usually brief. The characters are seen subjectively, through their effect on Jane. Mr. Brocklehurst, Mrs. Fairfax, Mrs. Reed, Miss Ingram, all may have private thoughts and secret miseries, but we know nothing about these, for we see only what Jane sees. "Strong feelings provoke her [Charlotte] to exaggerate unconsciously those traits which annoyed her - Brocklehurst and Mrs. Reed are the embodiments of malignancy which they were in the eyes of the downtrodden child - In one and that the most important sense, there is only one character and one subject in *Jane Eyre*, Jane herself; the rest, whether men and women or sticks and stones, are only the things that impinged on her consciousness." - Baker, p. 44.

MRS. SARAH REED

Mother of John, Eliza, and Georgiana Reed, and aunt by marriage to Jane, She dislikes the child and treats her harshly, locking her in the red-room until she is terrified, and finally sending her away to school. When Jane's uncle, John Eyre, offers to adopt his niece, Mrs. Reed cannot endure that Jane should have such good fortune, and lies to him, telling him that Jane has died at school. She confesses this only on her deathbed.

ELIZA REED

Daughter of Mrs. Reed. Willful and selfish as a child, she becomes more selfish and self-centered as she grows up. She betrays her sister's plans to elope and despises her. She develops an interest in Anglo-Catholicism, follows a narrow and austere daily routine, and eventually becomes a Roman Catholic nun at Lisle.

GEORGIANA REED

Daughter of Mrs. Reed. A pretty, golden-haired child, Georgiana is petted by everyone and becomes spoiled, spiteful and saucy. As a young girl she is frivolous and empty-headed. She marries "a wealthy worn-out man of fashion."

JOHN EYRE

Jane's uncle. For a long time she does not know of his existence. He does not actually appear in the novel, but is mentioned several times. He inquires at Gateshead for Jane while she is away at Lowood and later writes and offers to adopt her, but he is told she is dead. Later he finds she is still alive, and when he dies he leaves her his money.

BESSIE LEE, LATER LEAVEN

Nursemaid at the Reeds. Bessie is quick and competent in all she does and, though sometimes short-tempered, is kinder to Jane than most people in the Reed household. She has a sweet voice, sings Jane **ballads** such as the one about "the poor orphan child," and tells delightful stories. She is loyal in her affection for Jane, for she visits her at Lowood after her marriage to the coachman Robert Leaven, and brings her little boy for Jane to see.

ABBOTT

Mrs. Reed's lady's maid. She takes an unfavorable view of Jane and warns her that God may strike her dead in the midst of one of her tantrums.

MR. LLOYD

The apothecary (chemist) called in by Mrs. Reed when the servants were ill. A kindly man, he understands that Jane is in a highly nervous state, tries patiently to find out why she is upset, and recommends that she be sent away to school.

MR. BROCKLEHURST

The founder and superintendent of Lowood. His mother, Naomi Brocklehurst, gave money for rebuilding part of the school. To Jane Mr. Brocklehurst appears as a "black marble clergyman," tall and solemn in appearance and stern and harsh in manner. He inquiries into the minutest details of the school, encourages austerity and self-denial, and hopes "to mortify in these girls the lusts of the flesh." He counsels Miss Temple not to "feed the girls' bodies and starve their immortal souls" and quotes Biblical warnings against the "snares of vanity" - warnings which seem a little hollow as his wife and daughters appear dressed in the height of fashion. To Jane he seems a hypocrite wearing a mask of piety and charity. Charlotte based his character on that of the Reverend W. Carus Wilson, who founded Cowan Bridge School where she and her sisters went. She blamed the school for the deaths of her sisters. Brocklehurst certainly resembles Carus Wilson in certain respects. Some of the stories which Wilson printed in his publications for Sunday School teachers and their pupils resemble those told by Brocklehurst in *Jane Eyre* and give us a vivid idea of how a zealous and not very imaginative Evangelical might present religion.

For example, one story tells of Daniel R., who began by being late for school and later burnt his Bible. His "progress in sin was deep and awful" and although he repented he would never be forgiven. Another naughty boy spent nearly all his pocket money for a pair of boots, giving only a small sum to some helpless poor children. He did not enjoy the boots, "wept many a tear," and came to a bad end. There is much emphasis on the idea that God "can every thought espy" and can punish every ill deed, for example:

In your Bible you have read How he struck the liar dead; O! how shocking, if he do Just the very same to you!

Children are reminded to keep Sunday holy:

They who do this day profane Soon shall dwell in fire and pain, Never see God's dwelling place But be banished from his face.

To balance there are stories of pious boys and girls who would rather learn psalms and hymns than eat, and who perform acts of great self-denial. For example, "little George" gave his gold sovereign to the missionary society, modestly hiding it between two copper coins. A small girl aged four was told to pray for a new heart. She prayed every day, learned hymns by heart, and rebuked a sinner for profanity. She died suddenly at four and a half, reciting the Lord's Prayer. Another instance may be quoted regarding little Jane Brown. "New bonnets had been given at school to the children. A person, who doubtless wished to show a mark of her approval of Jane, trimmed her bonnet and made it appear more showy than the rest. She took it home and said to her mother, 'Mother, I can't wear this bonnet; I can't for shame put it on!' - and bursting into tears, she said, 'What am I, a poor vile sinner, that I should be better dressed than the rest." Soon after she was taken ill, but professed to have no fears of death ... 'I was talking before my sickness about having a new frock this summer, if spared, but I shall have a better robe to wear, than the one I thought of having - I shall have a robe, washed, and made white in the blood of the Lamb.' She died in great pain, quoting Scriptures to the last." (Quoted from W. Carus Wilson, *Youthful Memoirs*, Philadelphia: American Sunday School Union, 1829, p. 41.)

However many stories of good children are told, the same point about God's anger is always reiterated:

T'is dang'rous to provoke a God Whose power and vengeance none can tell; One stroke of his almighty rod Can send young sinners quick to hell.

Mr. Carus Wilson used "Suffer the little children to come unto me" as a motto and doubtless expected to do much good by his stories, but you can see from Chapter 4 of *Jane Eyre* how they struck Charlotte Brontë. [Remember that in *Jane Eyre* we see Mr. Brocklehurst from one viewpoint only, that of a frightened and angry child.]

There has been so much controversy about Mr. Carus Wilson's character that I reprint some of the contradictory opinions of him. Another old pupil, Emma Jane Warboise, who was at the school after Charlotte left and after it had been moved to a healthier site at Casterton, wrote, "His works of love and mercy were manifold. He was thoroughly sincere and unostentatiously generous. A kinder man I never knew." The bishop of Rochester, in an obituary, said, "He had the singular felicity of improving, if not anticipating in his various plans of benevolence, the leading ideas of his age, and his name has long been a household word in every Christian family. In church building, in the diffusion of cheap Christian literature, and in education, his exertions for half a century have earned him the blessings of rich and poor" (quoted in Raymond, p. 56). However, a modern biography, L. and E. M. Hansons' *The Four Brontës* (pp. 11–12), sets forth another opinion: "The school had been founded by William Carus Wilson, a narrow evangelical, vain, bigoted, and covering his sadism and love of power with scriptural quotations and appeals to the Deity. Carus Wilson, while the Brontës were there, was absolute master. The rigorous discipline and harsh teaching - intended to mortify the flesh and subdue the spirit (the only suitable training in Mr. Wilson's opinion, for poor girls with a humble future) - compared unfavorably even with the normal school of the time. His own writings testify that Charlotte, in her savage indictment of him in *Jane Eyre*, 'exaggerated nothing.'"

MISS TEMPLE

The lady superintendent of Lowood. She is a dignified and kindly woman. She entertains Helen and Jane in her quarters, listens sympathetically to the latter's account of her wrongs, and promises she will be cleared of the charge of lying. In cold weather she urges the girls to be brisk and to march like soldiers. She is evidently a person of some mental endowment as she and Helen discuss many books with enthusiasm.

MISS SCATCHARD

A teacher at Lowood. She is strict and irritable and finds Helen Burns' careless ways particularly exasperating. She scolds and punishes her continually.

HELEN BURNS

Jane's friend and fellow-student at Lowood. Only about thirteen, she is remarkable for her intellectual qualities and for her patient endurance of constant humiliations and punishments. She freely admits to her many faults, such as carelessness, untidiness, and absent-mindedness. She has a habit of daydreaming when she should be studying her lessons. On the other hand, for a child of her age she is deeply religious, urges on Jane the virtues of humility and forgiveness, and practices them herself. She was molded on Charlotte's dead sister, Maria.

MRS. FAIRFAX

Mr. Rochester's housekeeper. She is a respectable, kindly woman efficient at her job, but lacking a sense of humor.

ADELE VARENS

The child of a French opera dancer; Rochester's ward, and Jane's pupil. Adele inherited from her mother a love of finery and a frivolous nature. However, she is affectionate and teachable and with Jane's guidance and good schooling becomes "good-tempered and well-principled."

GRACE POOLE

A servant at Thornfield. Staid, taciturn, and inscrutable, Grace is supposed to be occupied in sewing on the third floor, but eventually is revealed to be Bertha Mason's guardian. She has a weakness for gin.

THE INGRAMS

Fashionable people, guests of Mr. Rochester. One of the daughters, Blanche Ingram, a handsome but affected girl, is supposed at one point to be the intended bride of Mr. Rochester.

RICHARD MASON

An old acquaintance of Mr. Rochester, who unexpectedly turns up for a visit. He seems apathetic, timid, and fearful.

BERTHA MASON

His sister, in youth a strikingly handsome woman, but vulgar and licentious. At the time of which the novels tells, she is dangerously insane.

BRIGGS

Richard Mason's solicitor (lawyer).

CARTER

A surgeon in the neighborhood of Thornfield. He looks after the injuries of Rochester and Mason.

DIANA AND MARY RIVERS

Sisters who work as governesses. They are at home at Moor House when Jane stumbles to their door. Full of compassion, they befriend her, take her into their household, and make her a companion in their studies and walks. They are well-read, refined, goodhearted girls.

ST. JOHN RIVERS

Their brother, a clergyman, well-educated, handsome, and zealous. Dissatisfied with parish routine, he plans to seek a more strenuous path to heavenly glory as a missionary in India. He is much attracted by the beautiful Rosamund Oliver, but, convinced that she would not make a good missionary's wife, he suppresses his feelings, masters his passion, and regards that mastery as a spiritual victory. He suffers mentally and physically from his conflict, but sets great store by iron self-control and believes himself to be ruled by reason and religious conviction. He admires Jane because she is self-respecting and diligent and gives her a position as teacher in the school he has founded. He persuades her to let him teach her "Hindostanee," so that he can review the elements of the language. He is an exacting teacher and drives her as he would drive himself. Insisting that Jane is "formed for labour, not for love," he tries to persuade her to come to India as his wife, admitting that he does not love her, but that he sees her as a worthy tool in the service of the Gospel.

He is offended when she does not fall in with his plans, treats her coldly, and still urges her to go. In India at last, he pursues his labors zealously, relentlessly, selflessly. The novel ends with the hope that St. John will die a faithful servant of God and go swiftly to his reward in Heaven.

HANNAH

Servant of the Rivers. Hannah is gruff and outspoken in defense of her mistresses, but honest and goodhearted. She is based on Tabby, the servant at Haworth parsonage.

ROSAMUND OLIVER

The beautiful daughter of a needle manufacturer, loved by St. John Rivers. However, he suppresses his love, deeming her not fitted to missionary labors. Rosamund was attracted by St. John, and Jane thought she would be a suitable wife for him for she was "not absolutely spoilt" by her wealth and good looks, but was good-natured, intelligent, charming, and openhanded.

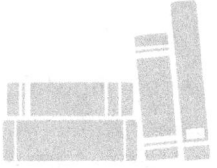

JANE EYRE

SURVEY OF CRITICISM

George Henry Lewes, one of the soundest of Victorian critics, reviewed *Jane Eyre* in *Fraser's Magazine* (1847). He was much moved by the novel, which he admired for its excellent plot, its vivid characterization, and its fidelity to life. "... reality - deep, significant reality - is the great characteristic of the book." It contains "actual suffering and experience," it is "soul speaking to soul." He confesses the book made him weep, particularly the account of Jane's childhood and the romance with Rochester. Jane is delicately yet forcefully presented. She is not pretty, she is not extraordinarily clever, yet "you admire, you love her - love her for the strong will, honest mind, loving heart, and peculiar but fascinating person." There are faults in the book, "too much melodrama and improbability," for example. The characters of Rochester and St. John are both limited, as they are seen from a woman's point of view only. However, Lewes admires (as some of his contemporaries did not) the character of Helen Burns which he describes as "eminently ideal and actually real." The style of the book is not elegant, but it is personal, "the written speech of an individual." The novel is a worthy addition to English literature, in Lewes' opinion.

Lord David Cecil, in *Early Victorian Novelists* (1934), begins by analyzing the limitations of Charlotte Brontë's character drawing. She is hampered by her very subjective approach. This affects both her female and male characters. Her primary female characters spring from "involuntary self-revelation." Jane Eyre, Caroline Helstone, Shirley Keeldar, Lucy Snowe, are all self-portraits, elaborately and fully drawn. The male characters are apt to be unsatisfactory, either too much like her heroines or unlikely mixtures of "violence and virility and masculine vanity" like Rochester. Neither is satisfactory or believable. In drawing her minor characters, Charlotte is limited because she only sees them as they affect herself. She can never, as Emily does, see each point of view in turn. While Charlotte has "a real and lightful vien" of humor, she fails when she attempts **satire**. Lady Ingram and her daughters in *Jane Eyre*, like the curates in Shirley, are heavy-handed and absurd. "Satire," writes Cecil, "demands acute observation and a light touch. Charlotte Brontë, indifferent to the outside world and generally in a state of tension, observes little, and never speaks lightly of anything."

Her vitality and her personal vision redeem her work. Its ingredients are "childish naivete, rigid Puritanism, fiery passion, and a sincere, deep love of nature." Her naivete is part of her charm. "It disinfects her imagination, blows away the smoke and sulphur which ardent heat might be expected to generate, so that its flame burns pure and clear." Her childlike vision, "so far from weakening the intensity of her work, rather invests it with a sincerity irresistibly touching and winning."

Ernest A. Baker, in *The History of the English Novel* (1937), sees the Brontë novels as late expressions of the Romantic Movement in fiction. The Romantic spirit is evident in Charlotte's feeling for nature, in her tragic sense of life, and in her touches of the supernatural. Her sojourn on the moors shows her to be steeped "in the Wordsworthian feeling for nature as one loving mother speaking to her children in the fields and streams." In her novels we find "a summons to the inherent seriousness, the tragic stakes, of the life we are all faced with." With Charlotte, as with George Eliot and Mrs. Gaskell, the novel begins "to speak for the soul, to sound the deeps of personality, to face the enigmas of evil and death." Equally in the romantic tradition are the "semi-supernatural phenomena of mysterious voices, ghostly laughter and omens and premonitions" which Charlotte borrowed from the Gothic novels.

Baker agrees with Cecil that Charlotte's satirical passages are failures, but, unlike Cecil, he finds Rochester convincing, though eccentric. He is "fully alive," full of "wit, eloquence and ... sardonic humour." In drawing him Charlotte drew on the Byronic tradition and her memories of M. Heger. The secondary characters are all affected by Charlotte's inability to see them from within. She sees them only as they affect her heroines, i.e. herself. "Mr. Brocklehurst and Mrs. Reed are the embodiments of malignancy which they were in the eyes of the down-trodden child," while Bessie, Miss Temple, and Mrs. Fairfax, who were kind to Jane, are favorably treated.

The plot of *Jane Eyre* is often bizarre, clumsy and melodramatic, but this does not matter, as it is "true subjectively," expressing Charlotte's own desire for liberty and self-realization, her belief in the primacy of love. "The greatness of soul which she put into *Jane Eyre* belonged to herself."

Lawrence And E. M. Hanson, in *The Four Brontës* (1949), praise the vitality of both plot and characters in *Jane Eyre*. Jane herself is particularly well delineated, a "real and distinctive little girl, with her sharp feelings and rapid changes of mood," while the child Jane and the grown-up Jane are absolutely consistent.

The novel is revolutionary in its treatment of love. Before *Jane Eyre*, passion in a woman was not considered respectable, but Charlotte showed that "beauty could exist in the desires of a woman." She is also able to express the tenderness of lovers through dialogue, while the "acid tang" of Jane's wit "prevents the love scenes from becoming over-sentimental."

Walter Allen, in *The English Novel* (1954), is critical of the plot of *Jane Eyre*, which he finds as melodramatic and absurd as anything in Mrs. Radcliffe's Gothic novels. He admits, however, that if it is a dream, it is "the dream of a tremendously real person," whose personality gives unity of tone to the work. The earliest scenes are perhaps the best, and comprise one of the most vivid descriptions of childhood in literature. The Jane-Rochester situation is based on Charlotte's relationship with M. Heger and reflects "one of the commonest sexual dreams of women: the desire to be mastered ... by a man so lofty in his scorn for women as to make the very fact of being mastered a powerful adjunct to the woman's self-esteem." Charlotte Brontë goes so far as to make Rochester maimed and blind before his reunion with Jane. He is completely helpless and humiliated and it is Jane's turn to stoop. "Rochester's humiliation is the symbol of Jane's triumph in the battle of the sexes."

Lionel Stevenson, in *The English Novel* (1960), points to the sources of *Jane Eyre* in the Gothic novels, in Scott, in Charlotte's own Angrian stories. The mysterious laughter, the hidden mad woman, the use of dreams and portents are a heritage from the Gothic novels. The figure of Bertha Mason waving her arms and shrieking on the walls of Thornfield is certainly a reminiscence of the Saxon Ulrica on the fiery battlements in Scott's *Ivanhoe*. As for the Angrian stories, "Rochester steps straight out of Angria, where he had been the Byronic Duke of Zamorna." Also Charlotte had, as a child, used in one of her stories the device of the mysterious call of soul to soul which brought Jane back to Rochester.

Stevenson agrees with most authors that the novel is autobiographical and that this is one of its attractions, as is Charlotte's ability to create mood and mystery. Her style is poetical, for Charlotte makes excellent use of **imagery** and writes emotional, rhythmic prose. Yet in spite of all these virtues, some readers reacted negatively to the book, partly because the love scenes are so frankly passionate, partly because Jane insists on the equality of souls in men and women, and partly because Rochester, who has had several mistresses and is willing to commit bigamy, is rewarded by a happy ending - marriage. "Jane Eyre was an intolerable renegade from all the standards of behaviour expected of respectable girls."

Inga-Stina Ewbank, in *Their Proper Sphere: A Study of the Brontë Sisters as Early Victorian Female Novelists* (1966) writes that in *Jane Eyre*, "the descriptive passages draw us into the action, the dialogue realizes the interplay of minds, and the **imagery** carries over to us emotion proved on the pulses." The dialogues between Jane and Rochester attempt something new in the English novel, avoided entirely by Jane Austen. They are direct and emotional. Jane's self-revelations are also full of power and psychological truth, notably in Chapter 26 where Jane describes what she felt when she realized she would have to give Rochester up: "In full, heavy swing the torrent poured over me." The "iterative **imagery**" in the Jane-Rochester relationship is also effective, as for example where Rochester repeatedly compares Jane to a bird and she sees herself as one of the "stray and stranger birds" to which he tosses crumbs. After Rochester is injured, the bird **imagery** somewhat altered is used for him, when he is said to be "a fettered wild beast or bird," "or royal eagle chained to a perch," who is waited on by a sparrow.

Among recent critics, Robert Bernard Martin has written the fullest reconsideration of Charlotte Brontë. In *The Accents of Persuasion: Charlotte Brontë's Novels* (1966), She warns us against a too great emphasis on the autobiographical approach to the novels. Charlotte was "neither camera nor tape-recorder." and herself declared, "we only suffer reality to suggest, never to dictate." She hoped to speak, she said, "the language of conviction in the accent of persuasion," and her novels deserve study as works of art quite apart from anything they may reflect about her life. *Jane Eyre* "is larger than life because it is Miss Brontë's vision of the totality of life, of man's relation to his heart, mind, loved ones, and God, and any such vision must necessarily transcend the probable limits of experience of any individual."

The novel is unified around the maturing and self-recognition of Jane and Rochester. They are contrasted, because Jane's training and religious principles keep her from making "gross errors of judgment," whereas Rochester falls into sin and has to be redeemed. His story is important, and rounds out the novel but Jane's is more central, not only because she tells it in the first person, but because we see everything that happens in relation to her. We come to like her and believe in her; "we trust her reactions rather than peering over her shoulder in order to form our own opinions."

The action takes place in five segments, each with its own setting: Gateshead, Lowood, Thornfield, Moor House, Ferndean. The structure is like a five-act play with two interludes in which Jane returns from Thornfield to Gateshead and from Moor House to Thornfield. Between each two "acts" is an entr'acte, a carefully described account of the journey, "with Jane looking forward to each locale with a mixture of pleasure and dread." On each journey she is alone and each except the last brings her into a new circle of acquaintances.

At Gateshead, Jane is "passionately self-willed," capable of terrible anger, though conscious of a painful letdown after her confrontation with her aunt. Her terror in the red room and at the sight of the "red glare" of the nursery fire testifies to supernatural fear and a high strung nature and she takes refuge in fairy tales, *Gulliver's Travels*, and romantic pictures. At Lowood she is as repulsed by the coarseness of Mr. Brocklehurst as Gulliver was repulsed by the Brobdingnagians, a coarseness which reflects the grossness of his soul, for he terrifies the girls with his pitiless Calvinism. The coldness of the dormitory at Lowood and at Brocklehurst Church are excellently described and are a parallel to Brocklehurst's coldness of spirit. For true religious teaching Jane turns to Helen Burns, who tells her to be patient and forgiving and not to rely too much on human affection. To Jane this is a counsel of perfection, and perhaps she is closer to Miss Temple, who on one occasion defies Mr. Brocklehurst and who encourages "harmonious thoughts" and "better regulated feelings" in her pupil.

At Thornfield Jane meets Rochester. When his horse first appears in the lane, Jane thinks she is seeing a Gytrash, but she has become less superstitious with maturity and her common sense soon asserts itself. "The incident might stand as a microcosm of the whole Thornfield section, with Jane attracted to illusion, then sturdily putting it from her." Even before the existence of Bertha Mason is revealed, Jane knows her relationship with Rochester is coming between her and God: "I could not ... see God for his creature, of whom I had made an idol." Her refusal to live as Rochester's mistress, her decision to leave him are "a heroic assertion of the sanctity of the individual soul."

In Jane's lonely wanderings on the heath before she is given hospitality by the Rivers family, Martin sees parallel with the wanderings of Lear, and shows by suggestive quotations that the play was much in Charlotte's mind. "In each case the **protagonist** leaves a home that he has been assured would be his throughout life, turns to a nature that seems at first to be friendlier than man, then suffers its pitiless buffeting, and is at last taken in to be sheltered by compassionate fellow men on whom he has no claim." Each is conscious of hurting the one person who most clearly offers love. In her relationship with St. John Rivers, Jane is offered an opposite temptation to that presented by Rochester. He offered her love without marriage; St. John offers marriage without love. Rejecting passion, Rivers would have her renounce the flesh. Jane wonders if God intended her to make this marriage. "Only when St. John involves God's name in support of a false ideal of marriage, as Rochester has done in the garden scene at Thornfield, does the supernatural intervene." Parallel to the destruction of the chestnut tree is "the mysterious voice of Rochester carried on the wind."

The reunion scene at Ferndean "has overtones of temporizing, of lessons learned, that give it a quiet autumnal quality" unlike the lyric rapture of the garden scene. Both Jane and Rochester have suffered, but both are now assured of each other's love. Theirs is a love between "emotional and spiritual equals," not an equality in a legal or political sense, but the "recognition that the same heart and the same spirit animate both men and women, and that love is the pairing of equals."

Whereas Jane triumphs over temptation because of her religious principles, Rochester is led from sin to repentance. This reading of Rochester's history Martin defends from Charlotte's own account of his character to W. S. Williams: "He is ill-educated, misguided, errs, when he does err, through rashness and inexperience:

he lives for a time as other men live, but being radically better than most men, he does not like that degraded life, and is never happy in it. He is taught the severe lessons of experience and has sense to learn wisdom from them." Unlike some modern readers, Charlotte does not exonerate Rochester from blame in the disaster of his first marriage. It was a conventional marriage for financial advantage, and Rochester was guilty of rashness and blindness. He is certainly wrong in taking a series of mistresses, and wrong, too, when he invokes the sanction of God in proposing to commit bigamy with Jane, for he is trying to "bend divine law to sanctify his own wishes." After he loses Jane, he suffers terribly, even before he is maimed and blinded. "Divine justice pursued its course," he reflects, "disasters came thick upon me ... His chastisements are mighty; and one smote me which has humbled me forever."

"The holocaust of Thornfield," comments Martin, becomes a ritualistic purging of his sin." Rochester recognizes the reality of the spiritual world and prays for strength to lead a better life. The stress on religion in the lives of both Jane and Rochester shows that *Jane Eyre* is essentially a religious novel.

Charlotte deals less sympathetically with the more conventionally religious characters in her book. Brocklehurst and St. John Rivers, both of whom seem cold and rigid to Jane, are linked by the common image of a tall column and by being compared to marble. Brocklehurst tries to curb "nature," e.g., curling hair, in the girls at Lowood, while St. John seems cut off from the soothing influences of natural scenes. Both are associated with cold, Brocklehurst with the literally cold Lowood and the loveless existence of its pupils, St. John with winter weather and with his "chilling' and "icy" moods. St. John also has affinities with Eliza Reed. Both are meticulous in their religious duties, but both sacrifice their family ties to their vocations. They may love God, but they do not seem to love their neighbors. In these three characters, Charlotte rejects the extremes of Calvinism and Catholicism.

Like Eliza, most of the other women characters are found wanting. Georgiana, Eliza's sister is a selfish, shallow, waxen beauty. Blanche Ingram tries to be exotic and romantic, but fails to charm Rochester, whose interest for her in any case is chiefly monetary. Adele and Rosamond Oliver "have the miniature charms of bloodless dolls and the triviality of the inhabitants of Lilliput." Both are amiable but unimpressive. Only the Rivers sisters have character and intelligence as well as beauty.

Jane painted Blanche and Rosamond and describes Georgiana as pretty "as if she were painted." Martin speculates that perhaps in spite of Charlotte's own practice of painting and her lifelong interest in art, she may have distrusted pictorial representations. "She seems to have regarded them with something of the mixed fascination she felt for the Angrian creations of her youth, as something to be both loved and feared, because they represented a kind of idealization that had little relation to truth." The illustrations in Bewick's *British Birds* and Jane's own paintings are thoroughly romantic. Only Jane's self-portrait is realistic, "with no defect softened." The contrast between them reflects the contrasting attractions for Charlotte of "the stuff that dreams are made on" and "her stern desire for a naked objectivity." "It is the eternal tension between them that gives the book its special flavor. The danger of over-reliance upon either the subjective or the objective, the equal peril of ignoring either: These **themes** so animated Miss Brontë's imagination that the result is one of the finest achievements of romantic sensibility."

Like Martin, W. A. Craik, in *The Brontë Novels* (1968), is opposed to the autobiographical approach to the novels, and states her case even more strongly: "The Brontës' biography does them a disservice with the reader, and invites him to read them in ways which, while not wrong, may prevent him from seeing properly what are their individual merits, or indeed what are their purposes in writing at all." Many naive readers, claims Mrs. Craik, are "constantly duped" by the first-person novels of Charlotte and Anne into thinking they are reading autobiography. (Surely Mrs. Craik is being over-pessimistic here.) However, unlike Martin, Mrs. Craik does not reveal many new insights into the artistry of *Jane Eyre*. She does make the interesting point that although readers identify strongly with Jane, because they have experienced analogous miseries, Charlotte forces them to be somewhat detached. She frequently addresses the reader directly, forcing him to think of himself and his own reactions. This is reinforced by the retrospective viewpoint, by which the mature Jane who is writing the book comments on the child Jane who is immersed in her rage or misery. Jane also comments on herself with detached judgment; for example, "Bessie Leaven had said I was spoke truth: I was a lady." She sees that while Blanche Ingram is striking and she herself is plain, she has more to offer Rochester. Jane can be similarly detached about Rochester, as when she sees that though blind and maimed, he will respond better to teasing than to pity. Thus though the reader is deeply involved with Jane, he can at the same time be somewhat disinterested.

Mrs. Craik declares that Charlotte has "taken great risks with her plot," for only the Thornfield and Ferndean sections deal directly with the love story, while the Gateshead, Lowood, and Moor House sections could stand alone as stories in their own right. Moreover, these three sections are realistic by contrast with the sensational and melodramatic story which revolves around Rochester. However, the book never loses emotional continuity, for "innumerable threads of association and construction link section to section and incident to incident."

As to the characters, Rochester is dealt with the most fully. Mrs. Craik is impatient with readers who think of M. Heger as the model, as though Charlotte could not "depend on her imagination, or ... adapt the material of life to her purpose." To "analyse Mr. Rochester's undoubted debt of Byronism does not go far either." What is important is that Charlotte has created a character who is convincing in his context: he "exists as part of Jane's consciousness," at once distant from her and close, who becomes more exciting, not less, as we know him better and sympathize with his moral dilemma. After tracing the stages of his courtship, Mrs. Craik raises a question which other critics have also raised: is the man whom Jane finds at Ferndean the same man she knew at Gateshead? Charlotte provides a number of links, the most striking being the comparison to Samson, which was used on the day of the wedding which never took place and again in the farewell scene, and which reappears in the Ferndean chapters when Rochester is truly "a sightless Samson." There are other links. Rochester is still in the prime of manhood, still sees Jane as an elf or fairy, and is still a romantic figure. The difference is that they now seem more equal and better in tune with each other.

Mrs. Craik also admires the characterization of St. John Rivers: "A finely observed study of a man who turns egotism and ambition to the service of religion." Idealistic, very good-looking, religious, he is nevertheless very self-centered, abandons his sisters for his missionary career, and shows his poor taste by his love for the beautiful but shallow Rosamond Oliver. "It is surprising that he can generate enough power to become the danger he is to Jane at the end of the episode."

Charlotte's style of writing is distinctively her own. She is almost always "in character" as Jane, only occasionally stepping out of character to pronounce, for example, on women's need to pursue a full life, or the future state of English poetry. She uses a great deal of dialogue and has an excellent ear for the "idioms of class and age." The outspoken servant Hannah, the respectable servant Robert Leaven, the elderly housekeeper Mrs. Fairfax are all accurately caught and set down. "Dialogue between Jane and others, especially Mrs. Rochester, performs many functions besides verisimilitude: it is not often naturalistic, it almost always convinces, and always has a flavour of its own." Mrs. Craik observes.

Earl A. Knies, in *The Art of Charlotte Brontë* (1969) follows his predecessors in decrying a too completely autobiographical approach. He hopes "to show that she is more than the inspired improviser and fictionalized autobiographer that she was long considered to be." While there are certainly autobiographical elements in her novels, Charlotte rearranges and transmutes her materials so that they show "a marked degree of pattern and objectivity." The first-person narrative has been disparaged by Henry James and his successors because the speaker cannot deal with scenes at which he is not present and cannot without difficulty or self-glorification characterize himself. However, Charlotte solves both problems smoothly. The background relating to Jane's parents' marriage, for example, is worked very naturally into the servants' conversation, and we hear the end of the story later from St. John. Jane is characterized fully, not only by what she says and does herself, but by what the other characters say about her (for example, Eliza Reed, Bessie Leaven, and St. John Rivers), and particularly by Rochester's comments on her and his trust in her. He would be unlikely to tell Blanche Ingram of his continental escapades. Jane's frankness, especially to Rochester ("Do you think me handsome?" "No, Sir.") gives us confidence in her reliability and helps us to accept the more unlikely elements in the story. As Charlotte herself said, "When we know the narrator we seem to realize the tale."

Knies agrees with most writers that the **theme** of *Jane Eyre* is the search for love; but he makes clear that it must be the right kind of love, "based upon moral and individual integrity," each partner retaining "his uniqueness as an individual," which "in turn requires a firm religious orientation." Knies traces Jane's development from her rebellion at Gateshead, through her indoctrination by Helen Burns at Lowood, and through her rejection of Rochester's offer to make her his mistress. St. John's proposal "is even more outrageous ... than Rochester's, for it involves a spiritual prostitution instead of a physical one." It clarifies things for Jane and when the couple are reunited, the relationship is on a more satisfactory footing. Rochester has learned from experience to value the right things: "Never mind fine clothes and jewels, now: all that is not worth a fillip." It is Jane herself who is important. Knies denies that Rochester's mutilation is, as Walter Allen claimed, "a symbol of Jane's triumph in the battle of the sexes." They come together as equal partners, "not as victor and vanquished." Jane says, "In his presence I thoroughly lived; and he in mine." "In their marriage all the conflicts of the novel are resolved. Jane is at peace with God and man, and especially with herself."

Raymond Williams, in the English Novel from *Dickens to Lawrence* (1970), notes that Charlotte and Emily Brontë, though very different in other respects, were linked by intensity of feeling. In this they were heirs to the Romantic Movement. Blake, Keats, Shelley, and Byron, all in different styles, expressed "an intense affirmation of love and desire, and an intense, often desperate apprehension of isolation and loss." It was sometime before this affirmation and apprehension entered the novel. "The achievement of the Brontë sisters ... is that in different ways they remade the novel so that this kind of passion could be directly communicated." This emphasis on feeling had two effects. In a century when men learned (partly through public school atmosphere and discipline) not to cry and to enforce a rigid self-control, women like the Brontës, Mrs. Gaskell, and George Eliot helped to keep alive intensity of feeling, and so preserved "a human world." Secondly, the Brontës helped to destroy the stereo-type of the governess. They knew by experience how their employers viewed their governesses, "repressive, unfeminine, dowdy"; "knew it in their own ways, broke it with a strength and courage that puts us all in their debt." *Jane Eyre*, through the first-person narrative, emerges as a whole individual, intense, alone, in complete and intimate relationship with the reader, who is absorbed into the narrative by her "urgent voice." Like *Wuthering Heights*, the novel has "tension and power" which makes it a truly dramatic piece of work.

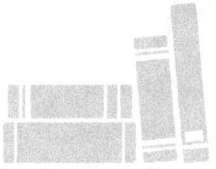

JANE EYRE

ESSAY QUESTIONS AND ANSWERS

Question: To what extent is Jane Eyre characterized by the comments and attitudes of other persons in the Gateshead **episodes** of the novel?

Answer:

> Mr. Brocklehurst: "'Well, Jane Eyre, and are you a good child?'"
>
> "'Impossible to reply to this in the affirmative; my little world held a contrary opinion.'"

While we do learn some genuine facts about Jane and her situation from what other people say about her, the above quotation should warn us not to take everything we hear literally. We need to sift the evidence and to consider the source in each case.

In Chapter 1, we do get a very vivid idea of Jane's situation from things John Reed and his mother say. From John's bullying attack on Jane, we learn that Jane is an orphan, dependent on the Reeds for everything she has, and that John resents this fact and constantly reminds Jane of it. From his mother, Mrs. Reed, we learn that she punishes Jane by excluding her from the family circle and that she finds Jane unattractive and different - unsociable, unchildlike, unnatural. She evidently resents her presence in the household. Our sense of Jane's dependence is reinforced by the comments of Abbot and Bessie, the two servants who drag Jane away to the red-room. Bessie reminds her that if it were not for her Aunt Reed, she would have to go to the poor house, and Abbot reminds her that she is inferior to her cousins and therefore should be humble and pleasant; besides, God might strike her dead in one of her temper tantrums and she would go to hell. The servants also underline for us the fact that Jane's recent defiance of John represents a new mood of rebellion. "She never did so before," remarks Bessie. However, we do not necessarily believe everything the servants say: when Abbot tells poor Jane that something may come down the chimney and get her, we certainly do not believe it, and we do not believe her either when she says that Jane screamed out on purpose to attract attention.

Mr. Lloyd, who is called in after Jane faints in the bedroom, does not exactly voice his comments, but his brusque and unsentimental manner encourages us to trust him, and we see from his questions that he thinks that all is not well with Jane's situation. As the day closes, the two servants again voice their opinions of Jane. Bessie rather thinks she is to be pitied, but Abbot finds her "a tiresome, ill-conditioned child, who always looked as if she were watching everybody," "a little toad," who could win no one's affection. The author leaves us to judge between the two opinions.

During the interview with Mr. Brocklehurst, Mrs. Reed tells him that Jane is deceitful. However, after Mr. Brocklehurst has gone, Jane hotly denies this and tells her aunt how she hates and despises her. Again we are obliged to form our own opinion, and we are inclined to think that Mrs. Reed has been unjust, especially when we see that she is really shaken by Jane's passionate outburst-shaken to the point of trying to placate her.

Again a change in Jane is underlined by something Bessie says: "You sharp little thing! You've got quite a new way of talking. What makes you so venturesome and hardy?" She has noticed that Jane is less fearful and more frank and demonstrative than she used to be. She admits to liking Jane better than the other children, and the Gateshead period ends for Jane in a hearty kiss.

In conclusion we may say that while we can learn from the comments other people make about Jane, we have to judge from what we know of them whether or not their comments are reliable. From unpleasant people, we often learn how Jane affects them; from the relatively pleasant Mr. Lloyd and Bessie, we have a better idea what Jane herself is really like.

Question: Choose one **episode** in which Charlotte Brontë arouses curiosity by some startling or puzzling event and then uses a delaying technique to create suspense.

Answer: An **episode** which well illustrates the delaying technique is Charlotte Brontë's narrative on the arrival of the stranger, Richard Mason. At first Mason arouses only mild comment because of his pallor and his somewhat un-English accent and because he is shivering in spite of a hot fire. This is subsequently explained when it is known that he comes from the West Indies. But what really is startling is Mr. Rochester's reaction to the news of Mason's arrival. His smile freezes, his face pales, he cries, "Jane, I've got a blow," and staggers - yet he pulls himself together sufficiently to show Mason to a room on the second floor. At this point he seems quite cheerful. Then comes the horrible shriek in the night and the sounds of violent struggle on the third floor. When Jane next sees Mason, he is in bed in one of the tapestried chambers, his arm soaked in blood. Left alone by Rochester to watch the injured man - both enjoined to silence - Jane voices some of the questions the reader must be asking. What was Mason doing on the third floor? What is the connection between this attack and the laugh Jane has heard before? Why is it that Mason now obeys Mr. Rochester like a lamb, although the tidings of his arrival apparently frightened Mr. Rochester badly? The arrival of the surgeon and the conversation that ensues give rise to further questions. Why are there teeth marks on Mason's shoulder? Why does he say "she sucked the blood: she said she'd drain my heart." Why does Mr. Rochester hustle Mason so quickly off the premises? The reader has to wait for answers to most of these questions until a much later chapter.

Question: Charlotte Brontë is always very aware of the passing seasons. Show how she indicates this in any one section of the novel.

Answer: The period while Jane is at Morton is a good one to demonstrate this, since a calendar year passes while she is there. When Jane is set down from the coach (Chap. 28), it is a summer evening. As the heath is dry and warm from the sun, Jane is able to sleep on it without too much discomfort. The next day is one of glorious sunshine, and Jane watches a lizard on the rocks and a bee among the bilberries. The pastures, woods, and stream gleam in the sun. After Jane has been rescued by the Rivers and has recovered from exhaustion, she and the servant Hannah pick gooseberries, a fruit of early summer (Chap. 29). As Jane's friendship with the Rivers girls ripens, they explore together the wild pastures and the purple moors, now at the height of their beauty, colorful with fresh bracken (fern) and summer flowers (Chap. 30). We are told that a month goes by and Jane moves into her cottage and begins teaching school (Chap. 31). Again we may assume that some time elapses while Jane gets acquainted with her pupils and their families. The day (Chap. 32) that St. John Rivers comes bringing Scott's Marmion and discusses Rosamund Oliver is "the 5th of November, and a holiday." (This is Guy Fawkes' Day still celebrated in England. On that date Fawkes was captured before he was able to blow up the Houses of Parliament.) It begins to snow as St. John leaves and "the whirling storm" continues all night, so much so that when he returns next day he has had to plow through drifts and is covered with snow (Chap. 33). After Jane receives her inheritance and divides it with her cousins, Diana and Mary are able to come home, and we are told it is near Christmas. While Jane busies herself with making cakes and mince pies and refurnishing the house, she contrasts the cosy interior with the "wintry waste and desert dreariness without." The girls arrive "chilled with the frosty night air," and in the ensuing weeks "snow, rain, or high wind" frequently occur (Chap. 34). Meantime Jane writes twice to Mrs. Fairfax for news of Mr. Rochester; after the second letter, two months go by and Jane begins to despair. She records, "a fine spring shone round me, which I could not enjoy." It is a " fine May-day, clear, sunny, and breezy," when St. John takes Jane for a walk in the glen to propose that she should go to India with him. The stream is swollen with the past spring rains and the fresh grass on which they sit is "spangled with a star-like yellow blossom" (Chap. 34). Jane is almost persuaded (Chap. 35), but the voice of Mr. Rochester calling her name changes her plans and the next morning, the first of June, we are told, she sets off for Thornfield in the rain. As she approaches Mr. Rochester's land, the green hedges and hills look familiar, but the grim ruins of Thornfield are a great shock (Chap. 36). After she has penetrated the thick wood which surrounds Ferndean, found Mr. Rochester, and had a night's sleep, she awakes to a sunny summer morning. She leads Mr. Rochester out of the damp and dripping wood into the fields; she describes to him how "the flowers and hedges look refreshed; how sparkling blue was the sky." They are married a few days later, almost exactly a year from the day when Jane fled from Thornfield to escape temptation.

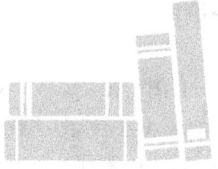

JANE EYRE

SUGGESTIONS FOR FURTHER STUDY AND RESEARCH

(Note that answers for the first three questions can be patterned after the model answers to the previous questions.)

1. To what extent is Helen Burns characterized by the comments and attitudes of other persons? (See model answer #1.)

2. Show how Charlotte Brontë indicates the passing of the seasons either at Lowood or at Thornfield. (See model answer #3.)

3. Discuss how Charlotte Brontë arouses our curiosity and keeps up suspense with respect to the curious laugh, from the time it is first heard (Chap. 11) to the point where Mr. Rochester tells the whole story (Chap. 27). (See model answer #2.)

4. Compare the characters of Abbot and Bessie. How are they used in the novel?

5. Describe the setting for Mr. Rochester's proposal in Chapter 23. What does it add to the scene? How do you interpret the blasting of the chestnut tree?

6. Show how Mr. Rochester's attitude to Jane grows and changes between his arrival and his proposal (Chaps. 12–23).

7. Describe the Temptation Scene. How is it made as hard as possible for Jane to resist Mr. Rochester?

8. Show how Jane's emotional maturity is measured during her return to Gateshead.

9. Charlotte evidently intended Mr. Rochester and St. John Rivers to be very different characters; at all events, they offer Jane opposite temptations. Do you, however, discern any similarities between them? Can you account for this?

10. Using the account of Mr. Rochester and the Literary Background of him (p. 34) as a starting point, consider the character of Charlotte's hero. Do you find him objectively or subjectively conceived? convincing or unconvincing? Give your reasons.

11. Compare and contrast the characters of Mr. Rochester and Heathcliff. Try to isolate the "Byronic" qualities of each.

12. "Jane ... is the vindication of all those who believe that life without understanding and love is a shadow, that the individual is more important than the circumstances, that the soul and spirit are indomitable." (Preface, Modern Library Edition.) Discuss.

13. Read Mrs. Gaskell's *Life of Charlotte Brontë*, Chap. IV. What details might she have drawn from *Jane Eyre*? (Note: The last two sentences of the chapter are inaccurate. The girls never went back.) Why do you think a libel action was threatened? If the Wise and Symington volumes are available to you, read the letters regarding the controversy at the end of Volume IV, pp. 297–314, and write a letter to the paper summing up your views of the case.

14. Read Mrs. Gaskell's account of Charlotte's relationship with the Hegers (Chaps. XI–XIII), and contrast it with a modern account such as that by the Hansons (Chaps. XII–XVIII), Laura L. Hinkley (pp. 55–79), or particularly good, Ernest Raymond (Chaps. 12–15). Can you account for Mrs. Gaskell's omissions?

15. Read Charlotte's Biographical Notice of her sisters which you will find prefaced to most editions of *Wutherings Heights*. Read either *Wuthering Heights* or *The Tenant of Wildfell Hall*. Write a paper in which you discuss whether or not Charlotte's evaluation of her sisters' talents agrees with your own. Be sure to give reasons for your opinions.

16. It is sometimes said (e.g., by Raymond, Chap. 16; see also Chap. 11) that Mrs. Gaskell as an artist consciously or unconsciously blackened Branwell's character so that Charlotte's beauty of character should stand out by contrast. Read Gaskell (Chaps. XIII, XIV), and any books you can find about Branwell, and try to decide if this is so.

BIBLIOGRAPHY

Allott, Miriam (ed.) *Selection of Critical Essays.* London: Macmillan, 1970. (A well-chosen collection of essays.)

Ashton, Winifred [pseud. Clemence Dane.] *Wild Decembers.* Garden City, New York: Doubleday, Doran, 1932. (An effective play about the Brontë family.)

Baker, Ernest A. "From the Brontës to Meredith", Volume VIII in *The History of the English Novel.* London: H. F. and G. Witherby, 1942–50, pp. 11–63.

Benson, E. F. *Charlotte Brontë.* New York, Longmans, Green & Co., 1932. (The Sidgwicks, for whom Charlotte worked at one time, were relatives of Benson's, and he recounts this phase in her life with a shade of **irony**. Full, well-written, and reasonably objective.)

Bentley, Phyllis. *The Brontës.* London: Arthur Barker, Ltd., 1947 and Bentley, Phyllis. *The Brontë Sisters.* London: British Council, 1956. (Brief but reliable accounts of the Brontës and their works. Miss Bentley is a Yorkshirewoman herself and knows Haworth and its environs well.)

Bentley, Phyllis. *The Brontës and Their World.* New York: Viking Press, 1969. (Contains 140 pictures of the Brontës and places and people connected with them. Miss Bentley gives a short, useful narrative of the Brontë story. A delightful book.)

Blackburn, Ruth H. (ed.) *The Brontë Sisters.* Boston: D. C. Heath & Co., 1964. (A collection of primary sources on the Brontës, including juvenilia, letters, poems, reviews, and reminiscence by contemporaries. There are maps and a linking narrative.)

Bradby, G. F. *The Brontës and Other Essays.* Oxford: Oxford University Press, 1932. Reprinted, Freeport, New York: Books for Libraries Press, 1967. (Tries to sort out facts from untrustworthy legends. Entertaining reading.)

Brontë, Charlotte. *Jane Eyre,* ed. Jane Jack and Margaret Smith. Oxford: Claredon Press, 1969. (Includes explanations of all allusions, notes Charlotte's occasional anachronisms, and gives quotations from Charlotte's letters and other sources to illustrate autobiographical passages. There are appendixes on the chronology of *Jane Eyre,* Lowood School, St. John Rivers, Charlotte's spelling; excerpts from contemporary reviews are reprinted from the third edition.)

Cecil, Lord David. "Charlotte Brontë," *Early Victorian Novelists.* Chicago: The University of Chicago Press, 1958, pp. 100–135. (Delightful and witty evaluation of Charlotte's faults and excellences.)

Chadwick, Mrs. Ellis H. *In the Footsteps of the Brontës.* London: Isaac Pitman & Sons, 1914.

(Visited every place connected with the Brontës and found out all she could about their doings and acquaintances there. Invaluable for reference. Many pictures.)

Craik, W. A. *The Brontë Novels.* London: Gethuren, 1968.

(Thinks the autobiographical approach has done a disservice to the novels. Emphasizes Jane's relative detachment and the retrospective viewpoint. Admires consistency of Rochester and St. John.)

Ewbank, Inga-Stina. *Their Proper Sphere, A Study of the Brontë Sisters as Early Victorian Female Novelists.* Cambridge: Harvard University Press, 1966.

(A study of the Brontës in the context of "female authorship" in the 1840s. Treats Anne as a moralist, Emily as a poet, and Charlotte "as an author only.")

Ewbank, Jane H. *The Life and Works of William C. Wilson.* Kendal: Titus Wilson & Son, 1960. Review of this T. L. S. XXL (Aug.) 484.

(A short account of the original of "Mr. Brocklehurst." Valuable for the light it throws on evangelicalism. Favorable to Carus Wilson.)

Gaskell, Elizabeth Cleghorn. *Life of Charlotte Brontë.* (Everyman's Library), New York: E. P. Dutton & Co., 1908.

(The first "official" life of Charlotte, authorized by Mr. Brontë. Mrs. Gaskell knew Charlotte quite well during her last years and talked to many other people who had known her. She therefore preserved valuable memories of Charlotte, and her book should certainly be read by anyone interested in the Brontës. It is artistically planned and executed. However, the reader should be aware that it contains some inaccuracies. Mrs. Gaskell exaggerates the conditions at Cowan Bridge, tends to picture Branwell as worse than he was, distorts the story about the lady Branwell was in love with, and underplays Charlotte's affection for M. Heger.)

Gerin, Winifred. *Charlotte Brontë: The Evolution of a Genius.* Oxford: Clarendon Press, 1967.

Every aspect of Charlotte's life and circle has been researched in massive detail. Not all her conclusions are good, but Miss Gerin has certainly brought together much new material on the Brontës.

Gregor, Ian (ed.) *The Brontës: A Collection of Critical Essays.* Englewood Cliffs, N. J.: Prentice Hall, 1970.

Contains an essay on love in *Jane Eyre* and other useful extracts.

Hanson, Lawrence and E. M. *The Four Brontës*. New York: Oxford University Press, 1949. Reprinted London: Archon Books, 1967.

Quite a comprehensive and fair study of all four Brontës. Useful for detailed references to sources. Contains a good bibliography. Edition of 1967 has a new preface.

Harrison, Grace E. *The Clue to the Brontës*. London: Methuen & Co., 1948.

Makes a case for Methodism as a "clue" to much in the Brontës. The case is overstated and the work is rather badly written, but nevertheless contains much of interest.

Hinkley, Laura L. *The Brontës: Charlotte and Emily*. New York: Hastings House, 1947.

Reprinted New York: Kraus, 1970.

Attractively written account of Charlotte and her sisters. There is a good chapter on the Brontës' respect for education and a reconstruction of the Gondal saga. Some inaccuracies.

Knies, Erik A. *The Art of Charlotte Brontë*. Athens: Ohio University Press, 1969.

Like Craik, Dr. Knies thinks Brontë criticism has been too much dominated by biographical concerns, and tries to reveal Charlotte's technical competence.

Lane, Margaret. *The Brontë Story: A Reconsideration of Mrs. Gaskell's "Life of Charlotte Brontë."* London: William Heinemann, Ltd., 1953.

Miss Lane reprints judiciously chosen extracts from Mrs. Gaskell's life and between them adds narrative and comments of her own. She writes well, and the book should appeal to the general reader. The illustrations by Joan Hassall are exactly right in mood and spirit.

Macdonald, Frederika. *The Secret of Charlotte Brontë*. London: T. C. & E. C. Jack, 1914.

Mrs. Macdonald was at the Heger school in Brussels almost two decades after Charlotte and Emily and knew the Hegers well. She is convinced that Charlotte really was in love with M. Heger.

McCullough, Bruce. "The Subjective Novel," *Representative English Novelists: Defoe to Conrad*. New York: Harper & Brothers, 1946, pp. 169–183.

Sees the intensely personal and romantic viewpoint in *Jane Eyre* as the new and unique feature of it; treats the novel as a personal fantasy through which Charlotte compensated for much that she lacked.

Martin, Robert Bernard. *The Accents of Persuasion: Charlotte Brontë's Novels*. London: Faber, 1966.

The title of Professor Martin's book is quotation from Charlotte herself, who wrote to W. S. Williams "The Bells [she and her sisters] are very sincere in their worship of Truth, and they hope to apply themselves to the consideration of art, so as to attain one day the power of speaking the language of conviction in the accents of persuasion." The author studies Charlotte's technical ability, such as her use of contrasting characters and scenes, to show her conscious artistry. Stimulating. Probably the best recent study.

Maurat, Charlotte. *The Brontës' Secret*. Translated from the French by Margaret Meldrum. New York: Barnes & Noble, Inc., 1969.

Emphasizes the role of the juvenile writings of the Brontës in their development as novelists. The many quotations from Ellen Nussey, Mary Taylor, Mrs. Gaskell and later writers make the narrative a little jerky to read.

Morrison, N. Brysson. *Haworth Harvest: The Story of the Brontës.* New York: Vanguard Press, 1969.

An undistinguished retelling of the Brontë story, with many quotations from Charlotte's letters. Mistakenly describes Mr. Brontë as a Methodist minister.

O'Neill, Judith (ed.) *Criticism on Charlotte and Emily Brontë.* London: Allen & Union, 1968.

Carefully chosen extracts from G. H. Lewis, Lord David Cecil, Kathleen Tillotson, Virginia Woolf and others.

Ratchford, Fannie E. *The Brontës Web of Childhood.* New York: Columbia University Press, 1941.

Fascinating account of the writing of the Angria and Gondal sagas. Miss Ratchford shows how the juvenile writings affected the writing of the Brontë novels.

Raymond, Ernest. *In the Steps of the Brontës.* London: Rich and Cowan, 1948. Reprinted Bath: Chiress, 1971.

In spite of a few mistakes, one of the best popular books on the Brontës and the places connected with them. Raymond's style is conversational and casual, his perceptions are sound, and he writes with drama and a sense of justice.

Shorter, Clement K. *The Brontës Life and Letters.* 2 vols. London: Hodder & Stoughton, 1908.

This book and others by Shorter on the Brontës have been superseded, but contain letters which may be useful to students to whom the standard edition (see Wise) is not available.

Spark, Muriel (ed.) *The Brontë Letters.* New ed. London: Macmillan, 1966.

The only edition of the Brontë letters in print, other than those reprinted in Mrs. Gaskell's Life. This collection should be bought by every serious student of the Brontës. Until the new definitive edition appears - Mrs. Spark's introduction is well-written and perceptive.

Spielmann, Marion H. *The Inner History of the Brontë-Heger Letters.* London: privately printed, 1919.

Gives the history of Charlotte's letters to M. Heger.

Stang, Richard. *The Theory of the Novel in England, 1870-1950.* New York: Columbia University Press, 1959.

Gives a clear idea of the literary milieu in which the novel was becoming a more respected form than hitherto. Has a short section on Charlotte Brontë, pp. 14-19.

Sugden, Kaye A. R. *A Short History of the Brontës.* Oxford: Oxford University Press, 1929. Reprinted New York: Folcraft, 1970.

Concise history of the family.

Thompson, Patricia. "The Noble Body of Governesses," *The Victorian Heroine: A Changing Ideal, 1837-1873.* London: Oxford University Press, 1956, Chap. II.

Discusses the heroines of Victorian novels against the background of women's general status in the Victorian world. Chapter on governesses is useful background for *Jane Eyre*.

Tillotson, Kathleen. "*Jane Eyre*," *Novels of the Eighteen Forties*. Oxford: 1954, pp. 257–313.

Introduction is good background for the novels of this decade. Detailed, illuminating study of *Jane Eyre*.

Wise, Thomas J., and John A. Symington. *The Brontës: Their Lives, Friendships and Correspondence*, 4 vols., Oxford: Basil Blackwell, 1932.

"Standard" edition of the Brontë letters, but containing many errors.

Woolf, Virginia. *The Common Reader*. New York: Harcourt, Brace & Co., 1925.

Woolf, Virginia. *A Room of One's Own*. London: The Hogarth Press, 1931, pp. 102–110.

Thinks women writers more likely to fulfill their genius if they have financial independence. Some penetrating comments on Charlotte's weaknesses.

Wroot, H. E. *The Persons and Places of the Brontë Novels*. B. S. T. 111, Bradford (1902–1906).

Identifies the originals of characters and places mentioned in the novels.

EXPLORE THE ENTIRE LIBRARY OF BRIGHT NOTES STUDY GUIDES

From Shakespeare to Sinclair Lewis and from Plato to Pearl S. Buck, The Bright Notes Study Guide library spans hundreds of volumes, providing clear and comprehensive insights into the world's greatest literature. Discover more, faster with the Bright Notes Study Guide to the classics you're reading today.

See the entire library of available
Bright Notes guides at **BrightNotes.com**

Available in print and digital wherever books are sold

IP INFLUENCE PUBLISHERS

www.ingramcontent.com/pod-product-compliance
Lightning Source LLC
LaVergne TN
LVHW021715060526
838200LV00050B/2679